# UP DADDY DOWN DADDY

## MEMORIES OF AN UNCOMMON JEWISH GIRLHOOD

While the incidents in this book are real, there may be some places
where some events or people have been omitted or misplaced.

*Up Daddy Down Daddy:*
*Memories of an Uncommon Jewish Girlhood*

Copyright © 2020 SECOND EDITION by Marlene Rosenfield

Cover design by Lauri Baram
Editorship by Dr. Dana R. Crawford
Printed in the United States of America

Paperback First Edition ISBN: 978-1-61468-0147
Paperback Second Edition ISBN: 978-1-09832-042-3

Still and forever
*for Dana Russell Crawford,*
*meine bashert*

# 1

# Up Daddy, Down Daddy

My Daddy shuts up in the early spring of 1952, when young star center fielder of the Boston Red Sox, Jimmy Piersall, moves next door. As for Jimmy, Mr. Red Sox, Shmed Sox, he never shuts up. Still a young girl, I figure craziness all wrong, Noisy and crazy go hand in hand.

Fact is, crazies dig up din like dirt. Even the tattoos they wear cry out for women, or wars, and who was lost. Desperate people drone on about themselves, all spit and sibilance. They plead. They promise. They bargain. They ultimatum you until you're ready to burst.

Only desperate crazies could dream up alarms and sirens—made to match the emergencies of everyday living. I recognize the worst kind of craziness: silence. First saw this not-o-silent killer in my second year of junior high, when dumb luck brought me this crazy next-door neighbor. Were it not for Jimmy Piersall, center fielder for the Boston Red Sox, I might never have known my Daddy, although that knowing would nearly kill me. For this, I owe Jimmy something.

I hear my Jimmy's loud mouth, blasting insults and firing orders.

Saturday: "Please. Grab that dolly now. Or would you rather see me put an end to my career by dragging the darn thing myself?"

Sunday: "Do I look like a freakin' moving van? I'm Charles Atlas, ain't I? I'll be damned. All the while I been thinkin' I was James Anthony Piersall."

Monday: "So now you're stupid on top of hard of hearing?" Tuesday: "Am I talking to myself out here?'

Wednesday: "Hey, who took my little girls? Round up my little darlings this minute or I'll huff and I'll puff and I'll blow my house in."

By Thursday morning, I just gotta get a gander of Piersall up close. "I'm going outside!" I plop down on my front yard, finger comb the grass, rip out a ripe dandelion, and peek over at the super handsome *Mr. Red Sox* standing in the middle of his lawn. His long thick eyebrows make a big letter V over his eyes. And I'm too far away to see what color they are. But it's his chin, long and low, that makes his face.

Piersall catches me staring at him from my front lawn. "Hey, you, I charge most people to look at me."

I hang my head, and keep it bowed, until he pipes up, "So what about you? Youse do any babysitting?"

Well, I hadn't, but I would soon turn eleven and figured it might be time.

"Babysitting? Sometimes, yuh," I answer. Piersall doesn't look old enough to be anybody's Daddy. My own Daddy was turning forty-two in the fall. With his hick wavy hair, this guy looks young enough to be Daddy's youngest brother.

Piersall shakes his head and starts roaring with laughter. "Next time will be your first, am I right?"

I nod.

"You want to sit my two girls for me, Eenie and Deenie, tonight?" What dumb baby names! Can I really babysit for two babies? "Are they twins?" I ask.

"Twins? Eileen and Doreen? Shit, no. Eenie's 8. Deenie's 7. Think you can handle that?" He shouts toward his front door. "Hey, I got us a sitter. Be ready in five minutes, you hear me?"

Who couldn't hear him?

I ask, "What time to what time?"

"Oh, say 7 to 10. You need me to clear it with your old man?"

"No," I tell him. "My Daddy will let me. But I'll clear it if you want."

"I want," he shouts and slams his front door.

Clear it with my Daddy? That's a joke.

The Daddy who OKs this stuff has been gone for a while. What my noisy neighbor doesn't know is this: I'm the girl who has two Daddies all rolled up into one. One Daddy's up; the other, down. "Up Daddy" bounces checks for hand-tailored new suits (an even dozen, he says, for the look of success), an Alaskan seal fur for my mother, a motorbike for his brother, wall-to-wall carpeting for my already rich aunt in Boston, and for me, a baby blue Smith Corona and for me, a baby blue Smith Corona typewriter to write my first novel. That I was in third grade at that time didn't matter at all; he knew I had the stuff of greatness in me, and he broke down sobbing when a guy came to take my typewriter away, still in its box.

"Down Daddy" has no bounce at all. He just rolls himself up into a dark, tiny little Daddy, so small that I often step right over him in the house. And though he barely makes a peep, barely moves, I hear him roll back and forth across the doorways. If he rolls toward me, I will give him a little kick.

I will. I want to boot Down Daddy out.

Maybe Up Daddy's the man for the job. If I could get him to put Down Daddy down once and for all, could I bring back the old, regular guy—the in-between Daddy I had as a little girl?

Oh I loved his Daddyness! Back in kindergarten, he scrambled eggs, skipped rope, bought me dollies, raked the lawn, wriggled his big honker and gave Eskimo kisses to Mom. Or else he'd pinch my own little nose between his thumb and finger, pull back his hand and then push his thumb between his two fingers. "Got it," he'd say, " I got your nose." "Let's see if I can get a quarter out of your ear, my dear." I went for it every time, feeling for my own nose to make sure it was still attached. When I last saw this plain old Daddy, I don't know. Second grade? No. Kindergarten.

All that was left to love after that was Up Daddy, who talked and talked until his throat went dry and his lips started to stick together. "Daddy, I'll get you some water. Don't move." I used to tell him.

Up Daddy was a delicious dreamer; he ordered a pre-fab doghouse. Down Daddy never got around to building it, let alone getting us a dog. Up Daddy gave me permission to write with crayons on the bathroom walls. "Go ahead, honey, write 'Save Israel's Jews. Win valuable prizes.' Good. You are a genius, you are."

But when my silent, Down Daddy went in to pee, he cocked his head at the ghoulish graffiti, pursed his lips, shook his head, and sounded it out syllable by syllable, as if it would make more sense, or be in better taste, when he broke it apart.

"Daddy, he asked me to babysit. "His cheerleader, I shout out: "J-I-M-M-Y (GIVE ME A P-I-E-R-S-A-L-L.")

He slumps in his easy chair and nods. Mom camps out with him on the matching chair in front of our wide open dining room windows. We live in a huge rich person's house, an Up and Down, with four bedrooms, three bathrooms, and the longest living room on the block. Beautiful bricks cover the outside. Top to bottom.

When you got bricks, you got money. Next to ours, the wooden Piersall house, looks just plain puny. So what that they have two more bedrooms than us?

"Joey," says Mom to the back of Daddy's head. I pull open the living room drapes in front of Daddy's chair. He scans at his crossword puzzle clues.

"What a way to mark the 50th anniversary of my Red Sox!" says my mom.

Daddy still does not look up.

"It ain't my anniversary, Irene," he says, and clicks his crossword puzzle pen to prove it. Five clicks. One fewer than the day before.

"C'mon. The Sox get the best goddamn center fielder in the league. Now he's my next-door neighbor. And picks my kid, my kid, to be his babysitter."

Irene cackles, lights up. Daddy draws back from the sulfur, as if she lit the table on fire, instead of her cigarette. She has built up a nice little mound of ashes in her tray, and after her final flick, she tidies it all up with her matchbook cover.

"Nu? You see the pitcher's mound I got going here?" she says pointing to the ashtray. This, folks, is what Jimmy will make out of the Yankees' pitchers." With that, she scoops up her mound in one swoop, flips over her shovel, the matchbook's cover, and empties it back into the ashtray. Pocketing her matches inside her pack, and slipping them into her housedress, she heads for the kitchen.

I hate to see her left hanging. So I yell after her, "Mom, think you'll get free box seats from him?" Daddy wiggles in his chair. It's as if a behind-the-scenes puppeteer has been fiddling with Daddy's strings. Puppeteer raises Daddy up, then lowers his head, and jerks it back-wards. With that, my Daddy raises and lowers his head. Sighs. Keeps his head down, pulls out his handkerchief and begins to blow.

What with the pucker of Daddy's face, the wheeze and whistle from his nose, and the quick swallows and sighs, he's bound to cry. He tries to distract me with a simple nose blow, honk, honk, but I'm not buying. I peer sideways to his cheek; catch a tear on its way down, and a fresh one right behind it. He swipes it up quickly with his knuckles.

What do *I* do with his crying? He is *not* my baby. I don't want to make him feel even worse, or embarrass him. Reaching over for yesterday's *Globe*, folded in quarters to the crossword puzzle, Daddy passes me the puzzle.

Not a single word has made it down or across. Is he saving his words for something bigger?

"Excuse your Daddy," he says. Then boom, Puppeteer pulls Daddy's hand taut to his forehead, a salute. "I'm going to get back to work on my proposal for easing traffic in this city." Up Daddy, the original author, had stopped at the fourth page, and left Down Daddy holding the bag.

We sit down for our dinner feast: orange juice, scrambled eggs, toasted rye bread, and kippers and onions fried in chicken fat. Since Daddy doesn't much care for dinnery dinners, we get to have things backwards. Yummy breakfastey dinners.

Mom hunches over her perking coffee pot. A cigarette dangles uncertainly from between her lips. Exhaling with a big fat sigh, she says: "Your Uncle Mucko tells a heck of a story about your Daddy's first car lot. Behind our first tenement house, the month after we were married. Yup. Fifteen years ago. This exact time of year. Daddy spiffed up two big ole Chevvs, one peppermint green; the other, who remembers?"

"Daddy sure could pick out the winners, right?"

"From then, whatever Daddy bought just walked off the lot."

"At Top Dollar Joe's?"

"Lechmere Auto Kings! The biggest lot in Boston."

"Was that really only ten years ago?" I answer myself.

"My husband wore the crown!" Mom smiles, stubs out her already burnt butt.

"Cuz my Daddy's made out of very different stuff. Right?"

"Listen, *meine kinde* (my child)," my Mom's pet name for me, "Tell Jimmy, from now on, you want thirty-five cents per kid, per hour. He can afford it. And you, bring me home a report on what's in the house. Furniture, food. Color of the Formica. Lamps, lights." She turns her hand over, and gives me a little *patchun tuchus* (pat on the ass). "Go. Get me my report. It's better to be early."

Report back? As if Mom needs to ask. I always report.

I cross the grass that separates our houses. I've got a big smile on my face when Mrs. Piersall opens the door. "Hello, there," she says. She is laundry on a summer day, all sweet smells, billows and bounces. On an invisible clothesline, she dances with her partner, the summer wind. "The minute he saw you outside, Jim said he knew then and there you'd make a fine sitter. Come. Let me introduce you to our girls."

She moves forward, then twirls back around, dancing still. "Gosh, I don't even know your name. Did Mr. Piersall ask? I apologize. Jim does most things backward."

"Marlene. My name is Mar-lene." I follow her few short steps into their regular-sized living room. Lit up from the TV in front of them, the Piersall girls looked like matching planets.

"Girls, say hello to your new babysitter," says Mrs. Piersall. "Girls?" she repeats, "Say hello to Marlene."

"A-low. Hi."

Meanwhile, I act like I've been babysitting forever, and nestle up to the girls. I ask, "Well, now, how do you like your new neighborhood?"

"Do Jews eat Spaghetti-O's? Our Daddy says your Daddy is a Jew," says one of them.

"Our whole family is Jewish," I tell the brats.

"Too bad your Daddy can't play baseball."

"Maybe he can," I say. "You know, my Daddy owns a huge car lot, full of the best cars ever. Top Dollar Joe's. Your Daddy will probably buy his next Caddie from my Daddy. See? You don't know my Daddy at all. He's made of very different stuff."

Each picks at her dirty brown *goyishe* (non-Jewish) Swanson's Meatloaf. I don't know which one says, "I love the stuffing the best. That's why the fried chicken and the turkey with gravy are my favorites."

"Why don't you have a great car if your Daddy has a whole car lot full?" The girls pop up, throw away their aluminum suppers, and announce, "Ta-da! We're off. Beddy-bye." Just like that, they leave me.

Whoa. What strict parents. I should've acted much, much nicer, played Go Fish, brushed their hair, put them in ponytails, and snuck them candy from my house.

Goodnight, goodbye, and hello to fat tips when I babysit again! To make those kinds of tips, you must make kids like you. That's what all my babysitters did. Next time, I will let them have candy, say, two, three times. On special occasions, I will let them stay up extra late. Maybe even tell a story or two about what my own magical Daddy can do.

Well, maybe not.

# 2

# Home Jimmy, Home Jimmy

Other people have a lot nicer stuff than the Piersalls. We do, that's for sure. I report that right off, along with my poetry, to Mom. "Redhead, red-shmed, probably peed in bed." Someday soon I might try out, "Sox, shmocks, I wish he'd get lost." To see if I can get a rise out of my Daddy. Or even a nice full sentence, with a few adverbs and adjectives.

Anyways, it's a cinch to babysit the Piersall girls. I get fat tips no matter what. In a few weeks, I was babysitting twice, three times a week. I will make a small fortune from the Piersalls. Jimmy does all the arranging, because he says his wife needs a break but she's too good an egg to ask for one.

By the end of July, I begin to call my next-door neighbor *Home Jimmy*, just to keep him straight from *Away Jimmy*, the guy who owns the outfield on TV. Away Jimmy bloodies his shirt twice in one game, it says in Mom's clipping from *The Boston Globe*, along with a torn-out picture of President Truman who had thrown out the first pitch.

Home Jimmy sputters at his wife and kids: putt, putt, putt, like one of those fancy mowers.

You just know Home Jimmy will turn up in time to embarrass you in front of people when he starts.

A good example?

"You know, the kid's old lady is a redhead, just like you, sweetheart," Jimmy says to Mrs. Piersall on their way out one night.

"Jimmy, honey, I am not a redhead," says Mary in her teeny sweet wife voice. Still and all, Mary Piersall wears her love for both Jimmies on her sleeve.

Home Jimmy shouts, "Damn tootin' you are if I say you are. It's why I was staring at you at the bowling alley in the first place." Jimmy smiles, nods his head, and says: "I saw that red hair of yours, darlin', and I was a goner." He beams at Mary, and gives her a nice peck on the cheek. Still, I know he'll slam the back door. I rush to my post at the living room window, where I get the best view: Home Jimmy will open Mary's car door, and then, bang, slam it closed every time.

He isn't mad; he's all about noise is all. And he's also about getting things done, and getting them done quickly. I imagine that's why Home Jimmy broke into his own back door twice, the second time with a sledgehammer.

Away Jimmy comes to life in Fenway Park. Nobody plays the outfield better. That's what the great Ted Williams, who plays left field next to Jimmy in left field, has to say on the subject.

Mom said, "Home run hitters rule the roost. They drive the Caddies. Guys like Jimmy, who play both center field and outfield, well they're driving the real muscle cars."

Boston loves Piersall; the teams that play against him do *not*. Crazy as a loon, that's what he is to them. Up at bat, he mimics the pitchers. When Satchel Paige winds up his arm, so does Piersall. Then he mugs, flaps, and lets out a squeal for both dugouts to hear. Other days, Jumping Jim oinks, barks, hee-haws, hoots, meows, neighs, clucks, and chirps. He takes longer to unkink than any hitter.

One minute, Jimmy's up at bat, leading cheers for himself and dancing the hula, while the crowd sways right along with him, and the next, he bursts out singing, strumming his make-believe ukulele. Jimmy smiles and gets a fluke hit when the ball hits his bat just as he's backing away. Five minutes later, pounding and punching, he's under the stands—in the tunnel—with his boss.

Away Jimmy has to change his blood-soaked shirt at Yankee Stadium three times this season. He gets fined again and again. "I f this keeps up," he writes in a letter to the president of the American League, "I'll be paying one of my enemy's lousy umpire's salaries."

Last week, my Aunt Goody, who lives just forty minutes from us in Worcester, sent us this story from *The Boston Globe*. Mom elmer-glued it to one of Daddy's shirt cardboards, and then read it aloud: "There have been few rookies in all baseball history who commanded as much attention as James Anthony Piersall, a 25 year-old product of Waterbury, Connecticut heretofore known chiefly for its watch making. In the case of James A. Piersall, there has been some-thing wrong in the works for a while."

*Paper, shmay-per*. He's okay by me. All summer, I think up ways to have Daddy meet Piersall. Finally, two Saturdays ago, Daddy promises me he would meet him on Saturday. Last week, Daddy went to pick up his check from his brother. He's minding the store at Top Dollar Joe's until Daddy gets better.

"Saturday, Saturday! Daddy. You promised. Jimmy's doing yard work. Daddy. Please."

"Only five minutes, right? I have my own work to do."

Next to the racket Jimmy makes, Daddy's eleven words may not sound like much. But to me, they're a whole page. "We're stepping out, sir," and with that, I hook Daddy's arm in mine and head out the front door.

Jimmy stands a couple of feet away, squirting his front bush with a bright green water pistol. "Hey, I clean home plate with this," he says, then tosses it in the air, wipes his hand on his shorts, and extends his hand. "Well, howdy, Mr. Rosenfield. My pleasure. I haven't seen you in the line-up all summer! Love your wife, heck of a gal."

Daddy hates germs and doesn't like to shake hands, so he nods instead. "Nice to meet you. Call me Joe. Please."

"Say Joe, you know much about growing decent grass? This ai no Fenway Park, but I sure would like to get some green here." Home Jimmy turns to face our lawns, spreads his arms wide. "What do you use for seed?

Daddy shakes his head, makes a fake smile.

Jimmy picks up a small carton. "See this stuff? It could grow a full head of hair on a bald man, eh? Then he picks up another, and starts juggling with the turf builders.

"Southern. Northern. They're all pretty much the same. It's the iron, really, that does the job."

"You a chemist, my friend?"

"Graduated Mass College of Pharmacy," Daddy says.

Jimmy picks up a third bag, starts juggling all three bags. "Pee-yew!

Well, doesn't this one's shit just smell?" He stops juggling.

"Nothing beats manure. Certainly not chemicals. Stick with nature."

"Where's your drug store, Joe?"

"I'm no druggist. Graduated Mass College of Pharmacy, but I wasn't about to be anyone's soda jerk. Never wanted to sit in a little fake box, inside a bigger box."

"You got that one right, sir. I'm outta my mind in the bullpen. You put me in the outfield, any outfield, then I forget I'm fenced in. Farthest thing from my mind."

Daddy smiles, extends his hand. Very good sign. Even a great sign. Guess it takes a chatterbox like Jimmy to get him going again. A regular Daddy, this talking Daddy.

I shadow him back across our lawn.

"Whew-ee, look at me," shouts Jimmy. With his hands down on the ground, his *tush* in the air, and his legs spread wide, he's a wheelbarrow. His head moves from one side to the other. "Get it? A goat. Them cashmere goats make the best lawn mowers. Can mow down an acre of grass a day. Oldest weed killers known to mankind."

"Daddy?" He stops, turns around to Jimmy.

"Stay away from weed killers, Jim. Poisons. Every one of them."

"Guess today a man has got to pick his poison," says Home Jimmy, and then chuckles. He's back on his feet.

"Not long ago, they were telling us hormone weed killers were safe. But put a few drops on a dandelion and it'll contort right before your eyes. Pull that dead dandelion out a day later, and tiny tumors along the roots is what you'll find."

"No shit! Oh, beg your pardon there, Joe. I can't stop cussing in front of kids. No more cussin', no more poisons. You take care now, you hear?"

Inside, I brag to Mom. "I think Daddy and Jim are going to be good friends. Daddy was talking a blue streak, weren't you?"

Shut up again.

Back on his easy chair.

"Joey? C'mon. Tell us what you think of him." Mom lunges for her Luckys on the coffee table.

Nothing.

I clothespin my nose with my thumb and my finger, and lay my own word trap with a pun from *Romeo and Juliet*: "A pox on both his noses."

Drawn on, Daddy's smile—like one from the Sunday funnies—is short and jagged. "Hey, I like him."

I give my Daddy a big smile. Mom holds off lighting her butt. "Really, I like the guy. Marches to his own beat. Just like me." Daddy, you don't march. You don't even walk.

"Course, I'm twice his age, but I could still run circles around him. If I wanted to."

*Then want to! Get up off your feet. Get up on you tippy toes. Tip toe Joe. Run on your tiptoes, never the balls of your feet. Play a shallow center field. Run, run back, like Jimmy. Run back to the spot where you think the ball might land. Don't turn back until you're there. Look up, look up, run back on your tiptoes. That way, the ball can't trick you. Look like it's bouncing up or down. Stay up on your tiptoes.*

"You can back pedal a heck of a lot faster than Jimmy, Daddy. I know you can."

But you won't back pedal. You won't. I can't make you; that's what I hate the most. That me, me and all my loosey-goosey love, can't make you move a muscle.

After my first day as a seventh grader at Newton Junior High, I come home to Mom shaking her head at the kitchen table, poring over the box scores. "Honey, how was it? Tell me about your day!" Much as she's happy to hear about my dumb Home Room teacher, what I ate for lunch, and how I said 'Hi" to three boys, she's torn between my day and Away Jimmy's.

I bite: "As long as he robs 'em in the outfield all summer long, who cares what *mishegas* (craziness) he makes. Right, Mom?"

"Such a young *pishingker* (a young boy), he is. Imagine him stealing the spotlight from the great Satch himself! *The Boston Globe* loves Jimmy. Know why? He gives the sportswriters something to write about, that's why."

Besides that, Mom has a Piersall no other Red Sox fan has: she's found a friend in Jimmy, a good conversationalist.

A Jimmy who calls her Irene, the Red Sox Queen, and shows her who he is right on her own front lawn. He imitates Satchel Paige; grunts like an ape, scratches his chest and his underarms. Jimmy clowns with Mom, talks baseball with her, even tells her weird personal stuff, like how he grew up.

"Ask me, Queen the Irene," I overhear him say, one afternoon while I'm picking up buttercups, "Ask me how long I slept as a kid. Maybe an hour or two a night."

"Shit, Jim. Good news this isn't."

"Even when my old man and my ma were going out, geez, I couldn't sleep for nothing. I was a bundle of nerves. Sure, I had fantasies, dreams of playing in the big league, making the catch that clinched a Game 7, with everything on the line. But that's not what kept me awake. Sometimes it was the headaches. Headaches so bad I couldn't get up for school. First I thought it was bum sinuses, then realized the headaches were much worse after a full day of yelling."

"Darn it, Jimmy, we had the same parents! Mine held hands all the time. Why? That way. they wouldn't kill each other." She breaks out into her naughty cackle.

"No, I'm the one who does all the yelling. Always scream at my teammates, telling them what to do. I order the pitcher on what to throw, screech to the umpire what to call. Every game leaves me hoarse, exhausted. At night, I lay awake replaying every move. I was maybe fifteen, no, sixteen, went to church and lit candles to the Blessed Virgin. Prayed and prayed. You know what for? Sleep."

The Red Sox Queen nods. "It is not too much to ask for, a *bissel* (little) shut eye."

"Still do pray for sleep, Red," says Jimmy, and then he imitates me raking. "You know, Irene," he says, pulling his pretend rake back and forth, "I'd say your hubby has a little trouble in the sleep department, too, am I right? Tell him to try vacuuming. It's what I do when I can't sleep."

He heads across the driveway that separates our houses, and stops. Like he's forgotten something, he starts to scratch his head. And with that, he starts makes monkey faces at me, and scratching himself like one, too.

"Ah, I love that crazy bastard. Again box seats tickets for the twilight doubleheader," says Mom, already in the car with me, and pulling out of our driveway. She waves goodbye to Jimmy, who is swinging off the pear tree. Sulfur fills the car; I love it when she strikes her first match in the car. She sighs.

"Oh just wondering what keeps him awake."

I wasn't sure which him she means: Daddy or Jimmy.

"You're not holding out on your old lady, are ya?" Now I'm sure she means Jimmy, not Daddy.

I am holding out. I am. In the past two weeks, every time I get up to pee, I find Daddy wide awake in the middle of the night, writing in air with his imaginary Paper Mate, mumbling out loud, pacing in the upstairs hallway. I have a small bladder, doctor says, so I pee three, four times a night. I wet my bed three times a week. If he sees me weave behind him on my race to the bathroom, I wouldn't know.

But I don't want to rat him out. Tell her that Up Daddy may be riding into town. That we won't be able to keep him out or shut him up. What I say instead is, "Jimmy's a real cut up." Then leave it at that.

# 3

## Paper Mates

"Daddy," I whisper, kneeling next to the sofa where he has pressed his face smack against the back cushions. Again. "Daddy," I say to the back of his head, "Have one of Mom's matzo balls." I've got one all ready for him, sitting on a big soup spoon, barely moving. Now that's a matzo ball: hard like a hockey puck. Doesn't even wiggle when I stoop.

"It's closing up," he says, and by saying it, I know he's back on his esophagus. He opens his mouth wide and coughs hard; by the third cough, he's gagging. A few seconds later: "Yup, closing up," he says. By that, I know he means, leave me. Leave me be.

I plop the whole matzo ball into my mouth, swallow hard, fling the spoon on the floor, and squish my *tush* onto the edge of the sofa." Here, I'll just pull back your blanket a teeny bit, and have a look." Good. Just that one little maneuver, and I've gotten him to roll back toward me.

Now I can cup my hands around his neck, and feel around for swollen glands, just like he used to do with me. He opens wide without my telling him. "Let me check your tonsils." I could use my index finger to keep his tongue down, but by the looks of his whitish, dry tongue, I know my finger would stick to that tongue, just as it does when I touch a frosty metal ice cube tray.

Faking cheeriness, I say," Fuss, fuss, esophagus! What do you say we put this esophagus on the very next bus?"

He does not say.

"What's Shabbat without Mom's matzo balls, huh, Daddy?" "Everything turns to sawdust in my mouth. I can't get anything down without gagging." He closes his eyes. "I see you, little bird. Hovering over me." Me, still his yellow bird, so-named for the sweet early morning chirps I made in my crib. Me, whose first word, light, had become family legend. No sooner did I squeal "Light! Light!" than my Daddy would put a blessing on my eyesight. "Light, light, a *gezundsah deine zight!* (God bless your eyesight)."

Today's Daddy does not bless my eyesight. He prefers what's dark, what's unseen. "Your old man has a bum esophagus. Nature's way of keeping me slim and trim," he says.

"Will you see Dr. Seltzer tomorrow, Daddy?"

"I will. It's at the top of my list."

I don't know which list he means. I have seen three: The Tuesday list on a torn piece of grocery bag, the Business Musts list on the back of a bill, and the Typing Paper list.

### The Tuesday List

1. Brush teeth

2. Change underwear and socks

3. Make one call

4. Write letter of complaint to Mass. Gas

5. Get Irene B-Day present

At the bottom are Daddy's instructions to himself on scoring: 5 points if he completes all. But why zero points if he's got four done? Mom's birthday came and went weeks ago without a gift, so I guess that means a score of zero. It doesn't much matter whether he changed his underwear, brushed his teeth, or made one call.

Although I wonder just who he would phone, one call, the whole item bugs me. One call is what you get when you get arrested. What has Daddy done that I don't know about?

### The Business Musts List

1. Order stationery and business cards.
2. Buy suits.
   a. Nehru collar Pierre Cardin town suit
   b. Saint Tropez ocean blue striped cotton

I didn't see any new stuff lately, so I figure Daddy got another zero. Lists one and two were a Down Do-Nothing Daddy list, that's for sure.

### Typewritten List

REGARDING Boston's Central Artery Project a.k.a. Billion Dollar Highway in the Sky

1. Spell out perils (from A to Z) of proposed coast-to-coast interstate I-90

   a. Apprise Mayor Hynes of unstable landfill contents: Plymouth Rock relics, glacial boulders, sunken ships, live utilities, slippery clay, and solid bedrock. Unwise to tunnel through such material.

   b. Question the sanity (don't use that word) of creating a forty-foot high, 200 feet wide, steel wall—between the city and its harbor. A Monster Wall for a Monster's Ball! Carbon copy to Eisenhower. Add personal note to the bottom of the letter: "Mr. President, please do not network America's highways as part of your idiotic national defense plan."

2. Remain polite and courteous. Offer assistance.

3. The Three T's: timber, tuna, and traffic.

4. Millstones and mirages.

5. Neighborhood plights. Plans for Chinatown? North End Little Italy?

6. Heated Off-ramps/a million-dollar idea.

Heated highways. Wow. I reread the last three items. All wows. Now this is an Up Daddy list if ever I saw one. I can't help but read it over and over. Okay, even though Up Daddy could scare me a little with his talk, I have to admit that I liked the Daddy who fired off his single shots: Bang! Bang! Bang.! And how I loved to hear Daddy talking aloud to himself like he were playing ping pong with an imaginary friend. Ping. Pong. Ping. I never knew what'd come out of his mouth next.

He could talk about a zillion different things. Like a Boston driver in traffic, my Up Daddy would zigzag his way in and out of sentences. He was really good at pairing words off into funny couples, couples that didn't seem to go together, but did. Take the day after sixth-grade graduation, when we all went for ice cream sundaes. Sitting outside on happy pink seats around the white iron table at Cabot's Ice Cream, Daddy started off with a teaser: "Ted Williams, Tennessee Williams, and William Carlos Williams. What do they have in common, honey?"

Not their last names. This I knew.

Daddy answered himself. "They have plenty in common beyond last names. Art and science, the physical and mental, the spirit, the soul. Same with the Miltons: Milton Bradley, Milton Berle, and John Milton." Mom says, "Two can play this game, Joey." She is smiling, covering his hand with hers. "Yeah. I'm betting Curley from The Three Stooges is really the same person as Boston's old Mayor Curley."

Daddy laughed, and so did I. Who would guess I could still feel the sweetness of the cherry from my sundae on my tongue. If I put my right hand on top of my left—just so—I can also feel my parents loving each other up, yum, yum, yum. Like big scoops of ice cream snug in a plastic sundae boat, they belonged. The belonging part, well, there's not much of that right now. But maybe. Someday. Maybe.

One thing won't ever change. I was the one whose first word was "light," and I can still see what may be invisible to everyone else. A regular working Daddy, suddenly smarter and quicker again. A Daddy lit up from the inside out.

When I get into bed tonight, I decide that we need a plan, my mom and me. As it stands, Up Daddy might just be a couple hundred words away. Truth is he's been leaving words all over the place lately. He must be cut off at the pass. He must. Forcing him too often to talk all hours of the night, he's already burned out poor Daddy's esophagus!

Can you fight crazy words with normal ones? Who's to say I can't get my original Daddy back, one sweet syllable at a time?

The way he was when I was a really little girl. Looking back, I can say that Daddy devoured words. On paper, in his ear, or fresh out of his mouth. "Please, sweetheart. Get Daddy his Paper Mate pen and let him polish off the crossword puzzle." After that, it'd be Anagrams. Acrostics. Jumble, the scrambled word game, you name it. He especially loved playing his word games with me right beside him.

We even had a pen game. I'd curl my fingers around his Paper Mate, and he'd let me trace over the letters he'd just put in. Or I'd pluck it from him just before he was going to mark some thing down. Starting his engine, he'd click his pen twice, my clue to jump in, nab his Paper Mate, and put it behind my back.

Funny. Now I do whatever I can to keep him away from the want ads that do not want him. Once Mom reads her box scores, I tuck The Boston Globe under my bed. And I have plenty more hiding places still available.

Still the question is: how far back can Daddy reach? If it turns out that he cannot go back to regular Daddy, then I will go back for him. Lassoing him with my love, I'm strong enough to bring him in.

Next morning, he is sitting in the breakfast nook in all his old hamsomeness. It's a long pause between his sleeked black hair, black and greasy, and his goldish, olivey eyes, underlined with one big puffy bag inside another, twice the size of his eyes.

You might think bags like these would look bad, but you'd be wrong: Pair them up with his long, thick brows and like two bold underlines, above and below, and they show off his Top-Dollar eyes.

And get this. Like his favorite automobiles, he has a cab-forward forehead; his *schnozz* casts lovely shadows over his skinny mustache and small, thin lips. Add that to the bright sheen of his hair, and the marbling light and dark of his eyes. On Daddy's face, you find not only silence, but also commotion, in one slow, steady dance.

Still he ignores his breakfast, two cold slices of rye toast with cream cheese. I feed him my words sunny-side up: "Daddio, watch this!" I clothes-pin my nose between my thumb and my finger. With my free hand, I point in the direction of the Piersalls. Then I lay my word trap with a pun from our favorite, *Romeo and Juliet*. "A pox on both his noses."

Daddy's smile, like one from the Sunday funnies, now looks short and jagged, drawn on. He plays a lousy foil; all he says is, "Shakespeare." He keeps rolling his thumb along his first two fingers. This may be his way of trying to get a small fire going.

"I'm climbing back into bed, Irene," Daddy announces. Mom asks. "Maybe call your brother first?"

"Up all night again." Daddy slides out of the breakfast nook. "It's Beddy-bye for me."

And we all know who keeps him up at night: stupid Up Daddy. This character has no respect for a family's clock. The night before, and the night before that, and the night before that, no "night nights" at all. And no more "Goodnight, my yellow bird, sweet dreams," for his daughter.

There's this, too: Piersall's moving in had shut off Daddy's goodnight switch, the way one house's TV antenna can mess up another's. Which explains why he has not left his own bedroom once to say his good-nights.

Now I'm the first to shout out mine from my bed. Four or five nights Well, maybe more like two.

# 4

# Top Dollar Joe's

"Top Dollar Joe is giving lemons away," shouts Megaphone Me. Eleven years old and already an actress. "Yup, you heard me right, folks. Giving the lemons away for free, by the bagful." With one hand, I hold the megaphone; the other, a five-pound bag of lemons. "Why are we giving lemons away? Cuz at Top Dollar Joe's, you get everything you want but the lemon. Those we give away for nothing."

Daddy applauds. Same as he did when I came up with the lemon idea. Me? I curtsey. Oh yeah. I also put down the megaphone.

"You hear those horns beeping, Marlene-a-la? See the people waving from Buzzy's Ice Cream?" The Buzzy Lovers keep crossing the street: Either they get their ice cream first, and then their free lemons, or vice-versa. Maybe six and eight years old, two buzz-cuts bop each other on the back, on the shoulders, and at the knees with the bags of lemons. Something to do while they wait on the cones. Not bad. A really pretty, red-haired, teenage girl keeps ribbing her boyfriend, "Hey, c'mon, you stand in line. It don't take both of us. I don't want them lemons to run out over there."

She makes a dash for us.

"How many bags you got left, girlie?"

Maybe I won't have one for you. "Plenty," I tell her. "Here. When your boy-friend's ready for a decent car."

"How many do youse put in a lemon meringue pie? Maybe I could get a bag for my mother, too, huh?"

"Sorry, miss, one bag to a customer. Oh, go ahead, take two." I am a genius at age eleven!

Heading back to Buzzy's and holding a bag in each raised arm just like a prizefighter, she yells, "Mike, look! How the heck will I be able to hold my darn cone?"

"Not unless you put one of the bags down first," Daddy whispers to me. "What a doozy! As for you, you're terrific! Now come. Take a break. Rest your voice. Have a little lemonade—ha-ha—to quench your thirst." He hands me a Coca-Cola.

"I just hold up the lemons, Daddy." Everything but the bat of my little green eyes. Shame on me.

Daddy tousles my hair, plants a kiss on my *keppie* (head). "It's not for nothing you been holding up the lemons! It's the future of Top Dollar Joe's you're securing with every bag. You, the brains behind my only advertising campaign! Which is a fancy-schmancy way of my saying thank you, thank you, and thank you!"

"Two dozen bags in less than an hour. Boy, am I glad Buzzy's went into business right across the street. And this being spring, the height of..." He stops, stoops down, feels around the big lemon crate. "Only three bags left; I say we bring 'em home to your mama."

All that from my lemons idea, huh? Not bad. Not bad at all." I take another bow, and then guzzle down my Coke.

First time I read *Wizard of Oz*, I figured Dorothy and me for best buds. I saw myself having so much fun riding bikes, changing our Betsy Wetsy dolls' diapers, playing hopscotch, cutting out our paper dolls and dressing them alike, skipping ropes, licking lollipops and Popsicles, and playing house, pretending to be someone else.

Back then, pretending might have taken Dorothy and me pretty far. We could click our heels together and then bring ourselves to the places we belonged. Me? I was definitely out of place in my own backyard. It wasn't because of Jimmy Piersall either. Where I needed to be right now was out of the house that housed Down Daddy, and be back on Top Dollar Joe's car lot. Where the lost little girl has her run of her Daddy's car lot and feels none of the new, big-girl hurts ever again.

Click, click go my heels, taking me back to a place where I can really help Daddy keep track of what he's got. Click, click: I'm a kindergartner again.

Starting with aisle one, I skip up and down the eight aisles, count the eight cars in each row, and see if I can spot any changes from the week before. Then I run over to Daddy's shed, and if Daddy's talking to a customer, I take his seat at the desk, and swivel, swivel, swivel in his chair.

Next thing I know, Daddy's back in the office, flashing three, one hundred-dollar bills at me. He slaps them on the desk. Another sale and it's not even noon. "So what do we want to move out next, Commander Joe?" I gave Daddy this nickname as soon as I laid my hands on my first Studebaker Commander Starlight Coupe, a bullet-shaped beauty. First row, front and center, this two-toned pink-Stude stole the show.

"If I'm Commander Joe," says Daddy, "then you, partner, will be my Champion. I need a full-time champion, sweetie. I'd be lost without you."

What I hear is, "I need" and "I'm lost." Why does he need me so much? Why me, say, and not my mom? Alls I can do is talk about the only Champions I know for sure. "Daddy, you have two Stude Champions," I tell him. Just saying

Studes, not Studebakers, separates a man from a mouse. "The green Stude in row two and the black in row three, right behind it."

"I forget you're a little girl." Daddy winks. "My little yellow bird." "Someday I'll be doing your puzzles, figuring things right beside you."

"I've given up on The Boston Glob," says Daddy, who says "Glob" on purpose, and makes me laugh every time. "Those puzzles, well, they're sissy's work." Daddy's *Boston Herald*, already folded to the crossword puzzle page, has gone wordless all week. "I like the big fat Saturday *Herald* best, since the puzzles take up a full page." Daddy clicks his Paper Mate pen, like he's ready to fill in the blanks. Instead, he hands me the pen.

"Go, you finish up your inventory out there." He hands me one of his shirt cardboards (he saves them up all week for me). Go, yellow bird, and mark everything down for your Daddy-O. Make three signs, too, could you? Write big: 'A Steal,' 'Must Go,' and 'Loaded.' Yeah, and one more sign: 'Joe pays top dollar. Trade-in today.'"I spring out of the broken screen door from his teensy office, and skip to the bigness of his lot. Always, I start at the first row, closest to the street; one by one, each beauty comes to life. When a customer saunters up and down the aisles, what he looks for first is the price tag. Not me. My eyes are on these jets of steel, inside and out, all fins and flash. Chrome faces and fender skirts: a beautiful lady outside, and an ever prettier one inside. One of my "Ladies" sings from her under-dash record player spinning inside. Another Lady Car could show off a little, show how her retractable hardtop glides right back into her trunk. Still another pretty Lady, taken in trade, keeps her driver warm and comfy with deep-pile carpeting. Seats studded like diamonds.

But my favorite Lady has push-button gearshifts, and a custom steering wheel with suicide knobs. Now there's a funny pair of words, a suicide next to a knob. Still, what a pretty *punim* (face)on this Stude, even with its teeth in shiny chrome braces. This here grill puts every other grill to shame. Except for the huge smile on the front of that two-toned lemon-and-lime Stude Daddy sold the year before. That baby took my breath away. Before that was the Starlight coupe, a ringer on anyone's lot.

I grab Daddy's Paper Mate from my pocket, and begin my weekly count, from right to left (counting left to right, Daddy says, throws off your inventory;

your eyes see what your mind thinks is still there: Chrome catches the light and blinds you, so you gotta be sure of what's left). Chevy Bel Air, throwing its red, yellow, and orange flames all around its huge cat eyes. Two-seat, red Ford Thunderbird, on fire with its redness.

Next is my favorite Ford: a purple Crown Victoria, which Daddy says may belong to me some day, since it takes a princess to appreciate purple. The Merc, 2-door, bonnet blue, and its cousin, the stinky steel blue Ford coupe. Next to it a Caddie DeVille, jet black. And next to that, a white '50 Pontiac Chieftan. White's no color at all, really. Yucky old Olds—also white—taken in trade, and taking up space next to it.

"Buicks, Oldsmobiles, and Pontiacs, oh my. Buicks, Oldsmobiles and Pontiacs, oh my," I sing. Quick call for an ambulance: Pontiac attack, straight to my heart. And it's then that I spot an intruder in our lot: a big, old, powder-blue Cadillac convertible with a wraparound windshield, rakish tail fins, giant red tail-lights, and sharp pointy bumpers. I run back to the office.

"Daddy, Daddy, where'd you get the Caddie?"

Daddy's pacing around his box of an office. "It's always a rhyme with you, my little yellow bird. Bought the Caddie for your Uncle Jim. He's picking it up Monday."

"It looks like a weapon," I tell him.

"That it does, honey. That it does. Most of the folks out there want style. The big guys at General Motors say safe-looking cars appeal only to squares. Well, call me a square, then, and while you're at it, call my customers square, too. Top Dollar Joe won't sell any car—won't touch a trade-in either—that is not knee deep in rubber."

Knee deep in rubber. That's car talk for tires.

Now me, what I'm knee deep in is loving my Daddy. Not only because he won't sell a car with bad tires, but also because he won't sell a bad car period. And he doesn't shove a car down someone's throat. None of this, "C'mon, take it for a ride." Or "Nice to see someone appreciate a fine automobile, sir. Don't see that too much. You, sir, have an eye for finery and I want to make sure I put you in a car befitting your stature." Which is why it took me two whole months to convince

Daddy to let me do the Lemons Giveaway. He kind of saw it as a gimmick, a cheap car dealer's trick, even though he didn't say it, I knew.

My Uncle Mucko says the competition spray their cars with new car smell. And use flat tire pumper-upper first thing in the morning on just about every car.

But not Top Dollar Joe. No sir-ee.

"Nothing sells a car better than the car itself," my Daddy says.

I ask, "How come you don't say 'just take a little ride in this baby?'"

"That's not the kind of stuff I'm made of, that's why. I don't push anyone; I let my cars do the talking. 'Hey, you, you should own me.' Or, 'Where ya been all my life, stranger? We belong together,'" Daddy grins, shakes his head up and down.

"I love how you talk. Your words are all colors, like the little orange, red, blue, green, and yellow triangle flags out there on the lot. Like them, all breezy and bright."

"Sweetie, it doesn't take a poet to know who's buying and who ain't. My cars talk to the customers, or they keep their mouth shut and rot on the lot. Lucky for me there's plenty of talking cars."

When we're on a road trip, say, and we pass a used car lot, I am the first to point out Daddy's pet peeve: the Like New scrawled across the windshield. "Huh!" I call it even before Daddy. "Weasel words, weasel words! Daddy, the whole front row's like new.

"It was the great Teddy Roosevelt who coined the phrase, 'weasel words.' Have I told you that already? Oh well. It's worth a second telling. Like a weasel eats and empties the egg without breaking the shell, so do weasel words suck out the truth. A car? It's either new or it's not. No such thing as like."

I spot a customer before Daddy does. "Hey, Daddy-i-o, quick! There's another live one." The wife has a huge pregnant belly. They'll be buying for sure.

He jumps forward. I stay behind. I know the drill. What he will say is, "Hello, there, I'm Joe. Top Dollar Joe." Again: "Top Dollar Joe." He says it like he's the most important person in the whole world …that he has a name that matters. I swear, anyone who meets Top Dollar Joe won't forget him, even if they don't buy a car from him. He will send that name right through you, and it'll bounce back from you to him, and back again. Ready to bop the next customer right over the head. You buy a car from Top Dollar Joe, a man of three mighty words, and for a very long, long time after you leave the lot, you will still have his name with you.

The pregnant woman's husband is circling the car, giving the tires a little kick. He'll know "knee deep in rubber" even if he doesn't use our special language. The tire kick is Daddy's exit: "You take your time. I'm inside with my little girl if you have any questions. If you want to take it for a ride, just give a holler." That's it.

"Some folks," explains Daddy soon as he sits back down at his desk, "get the willies. If they see a salesman headed their way, they'll walk the other way, and shout, 'I'm just looking.' No one wants a salesman trying to sell them a car. They want to believe they bought it all by themselves. Those folks? The only wheels that they'll be buying are the four on a baby stroller. Knee deep in diapers and all."

"But one day they'll be back at Top Dollar Joe's again, right?"

"Right, right, God bless your eyesight!" And he jumps up, squeezes my head, and kisses both my eyes. "And what does Top Dollar Joe do when someone interrupts with 'I'm-just-looking?'"

"You tell them who you are. Top Dollar Joe. You say it like it's your first name, middle, and last. Then you offer your hand."

"And step aside." Daddy sweeps his arm in a big arc, and says, "Go right ahead. Take all the time you need. I'll be in my office."

Sometimes, walking away, he will add, "If you're looking for one with ice, give a holler." Not many cars have air conditioning, so I think Daddy is very smart to tell them when there's ice.

We wait in Daddy's office for a signal. Used to be, he'd take a drink. Now great Saturdays on his lot are extra great: Daddy won't drink anything but Coke in front of me anymore. His drinking was perplexing since Jewish men are not drinkers. That's what mom read in *Woman's Day*.

Anyway, until I caught him, he'd been sneaking into the bathroom for a "quick, cold one," and coming out all smelly.

Smell is a thing you can't ignore. Only once, on a trade that some lady's dog threw up in, did Top Dollar Joe let me sprinkle a little of his Old Spice on the seats. I love to keep the beauties smelling sweet, so I get permission to drop a little of my apple juice or cherry Kool-Aid above the accelerator, where no one will see it. I so like to my keep my inventory smelling good, especially since, outside of this car lot, I can't fix up or change the smells. No mistaking a fishy smell for anything else. The sneaky, stinky smell of a drunk for the sweet smell of a freshly Johnson baby-powdered baby's *tush*. One whiff of my Bubbeh's *challah* (braided bread) and I'm a goner.

A goner. When I hit my next birthday, I will click my heels again and return to Top Dollar Joe's, and see that it has outgrown its lot. Only a year after that, one scrawny year, I'll click again and find that Daddy's car lot will have shrunk way back in size, but not his drinking. That'd fill a murky lake. At first he'll wade in up to his waist. His bouncing in place could have kept him there, there in one safe spot.

But a Daddy who stays still is not the Daddy I have, so he begins flailing his arms and legs, thrashing like crazy. The worst thing he could do. If he'd only relax his arms, he'd float. But no. One minute, he's knee deep in sadness; next one, he's knee-deep in quicksand. Yup, so knee deep that no click of my heels, of anyone's heels, can pull him up, up and up, out of the muck.

One day there'll be no place like Joe's. No, no place at all like Top Dollar Joe's, because he might be a goner, too. Can he dig himself out? I don't know. Years and years later, I'd remember him telling me how he had dug himself out, way back in college. Not one time, but ten times, ten different digs.

Let me tell you the story of Daddy's first dig in Boston, Massachusetts. Not to be confused with the story of the city's forever famous Big Dig. For when my Daddy dug in, he dug right in to the stuff he was made of. His dig made the Big Dig small; his dig made the Big Dig no real dig at all.

# 5

# Dugouts

Like the little old lady who stuffs wads of children into her shoe, and calls it home, Boston's belly swells in late summer with college students. Just before Labor Day, they limber up, swagger, steady themselves, and dash through Boston, a city made for marathons.

Daddy tells me about his days at Massachusetts College of Pharmacy. When he was a frosh there, he made a run for the Watertown Lecture Hall for his orientation. Inside, he headed not for the interior of that hall, but for the stairwell to bring him to the bowels of the building.

With his father dead, his mother and little sister visiting family in England, his two older brothers at work, Joe's free to do what he wants. And what he wants to do most is find a restroom with at least two urinals and three private stalls.

He finds one with twice that many. He'll have more than enough time, privacy and anonymity to do his dirty work. Inside the stall he sits, pants zipped up and belted. Joe rolls up his white cuffs and uncaps his fountain pen. At the bottom of his right pinkie finger, he pushes the nib in the pad below his knuckle, and begins to carve out a capital K. The three lines that form the letter fill with blood, but Joe's prepared.

He wads up toilet paper, blots a half-dozen times, pushes out the stall door, and lathers up the freshly cut K. He rinses in barely tepid water. He can't afford to wait for the hot.

Safe again in his stall, he retraces the singular line, the backbone of the letter. Digs deeper with his graduation gift, a Paper Mate fountain pen, lets it drops, frisks the space to his right for the toilet paper. As gently as he can manage, he takes hold of the tail and unrolls it with the reverence of a boy scout for the flag. Darn single ply industrial, as flimsy and useless as, well, toilet paper. No way can he coax the roller past the third perforation.

He counts out an even dozen three-sheeters. Next time, he will wad up fifteen pieces, three per knuckle, tuck them into his belt, and be ready for blood blots. He retraces the long vertical line of the K three times, each time drawing the nib quicker and deeper, and nodding his head twice for yes, goes for the two diagonals that complete the letter. He need blot only once to see the skinny shallow red pool signal ripeness.

Next time, he vows to come with a roll of pre-cut toilet paper. Fold them in tin foil, Aha, a foil that foils. After all, how hard would it be to filch, say, a packet of sterile gauze pads, from this place? With a week or two in between, he expects he'll have both hands done by Thanksgiving. With his left hand in a fist, he punches open the stall door, hears applause high above, and figures the welcome's over.

The clop, clop, clop tells him the other freshmen are making their way out of the auditorium. All that awaits Joe now is a clean getaway.

He makes his way up the stairs, and falls in with a few dozen departing classmates. No, they'll never be mates; no, they're not made of the same stuff. They're soft, inside and out. And they don't do nasty things to their hands. After all, what pharmacy would hire a man whose fingers are lettered, whose two words say something to him alone. No, says Joe, these prissy pussies will keep their hands busy, busy, busy, filling beakers, not fingers, with blue liquids, not India ink.

Mass College of Pharmacy is only a block and three stops on the "B" line from home, where he'll run a hot bath. He breathes in deeply, and exhales with a sigh. He can almost smell the heated vapor fill the black and white tiled bathroom in his mother's home.

The plan is for Joe to go to school for eighteen months, walk off with his pharmacist's license, and say, "Only soda jerks belong behind drug store counters." He'll be invited to interview, and remain careful to keep the contents on his fingers hidden from the president, and get himself an executive position. When his brain gets cooking and his plans are set on paper, certain people will get wind of him, seek him out. Never question what stuff he's made of.

He stands five-feet ten, with perfect posture, and once he tucks his jaw in, you see his face clearer. His hooked nose sets his grin and gray-green eyes into greater relief. His clear complexion and small pores give him gentility. Oddly, facial hair grows so slowly that he shaves only twice a week, while what tops his head sprouts wildly. White shirts (no starch, please) set off his olive skin, and once or twice, he's been taken for a Greek or an Arab. Once his ship comes in, no one will give a damn about his lettered knuckles.

But just in case any nosey parkers stare him down, he makes plans for the hands, too. He practices and poses. He turns to one side, then the other. He likes how his hands look in the full-length mirror as his fingers thread and lock behind his back, and presto, his chin rises along with his confidence. Full frontal, his hands fan out from his hips, palms up, as if to say, "I ain't movin'." He can sit on his hands for nearly an hour until the numbness sets in. He gets better and better with practice. At the dinner table, he's mastered cutting his steak with his knuckles clenched downward, safely out of sight like indecent elbows.

I learned my first few letters right on Daddy's hands. I sounded out the two wacky words on those knuckles. I don't know why he picked such a small space. Back in second grade, we were allowed to write on a wall covered with Kraft paper. I couldn't believe how good it felt to fill up a huge space with as many letters as you could make.

I don't remember how old I was when I began to see the world as letters on surfaces. I got my start in Mrs. Dubb's class.

Really, things were out there everywhere just waiting to be written on. Traffic signs, streets, signs in stores, and signs outside them. Cigarette packs, newspapers, greeting cards, pads of paper, doorways, parking lots, crossword puzzles, buildings, houses, cabs, buses, trucks, blimps, even airplanes. Not to mention sky, where you could never run out of writing space.

Come to think of it, what about all the words on surfaces you can't see? Private diaries, torn-up telegrams, top-secret stuff, love letters tucked away in dresser drawers. You could even stuff a teensy piece of paper into a Coke bottle and send it afloat. Your message might change the life of a man stranded on a desert island. Sentence-maker, messenger, you must gather up all the words you hear, read and see, stuff them inside you, and wait for the right kind of scrabble board to spill them out.

But here's what nags at me. What made Daddy settle for such small surfaces as knuckles? How did he ever decide which two words he'd live with forever? What would my two words be? "Duck" and "Cover"; "Mutt" and "Jeff"; "Live" and "Learn"; "Kiss" and "Tell"; "Bugs" and "Bunny"; "Howdy" and "Doody"; "Spic" and "Span,""Tom" and "Jerry"; "Tubby" and "Lulu?" Why not "Tragic" and Comic?" Nope. When I turn 21, there'll be 9 letters tattooed on my hands: "Paper" on my left hand; "Mate" on my right.

Classes began the day after orientation. Frosh Joe Rosenfield arrives two hours early for his first Intro to Pharmacology class. He sprints to his stall. But before he opens the stall door, he turns on the faucet, rolls up his sleeves, scours his hands with Borax three or four times, inspects his nails (yup, clean), and blots up with the clean hanky he'd bleached the night before. With a box of Johnson & Johnson cotton balls in one hand, he uses his hanky wrapped hand to pull open the stall door. Once safely inside, he flushes twice, sits on the toilet fully clothed, and, tattoos an "O" below the first knuckle of his (RIGHT OR LEFT) middle finger on his (right or left hand). "Oh," he giggles at his own trope, "O is such a cinch. I'm going for the second O."

Same drill. Carve out with the Paper Mate, blot, repeat. One continuous stroke, a circle, much quicker and cleaner than nearly every letter he'll need, except the "C."

Funny, how I pick and choose my miracles. I don't see any burning bushes, any parting seas. Never saw a whale inhale a boy, or a great grandma give birth. But I do believe my Daddy's own little creation myth. He would not need seven days to finish his work.

Daddy's scored two easy runs off the letter "O." Then again, he was only responsible for bringing eight letters to life on a much smaller canvas, just a knuckle, not a universe.

He tells his story as if it happened to someone else, a fictional frosh named Joe who arrives two hours early for his first pharmacology class. He sprints to his stall. But before he opens the stall door, he turns on the faucet, rolls up his sleeves, scours his hands with Borax three or four times, inspects his nails (yup, clean), and blots up with the clean hanky he'd bleached the night before.

Same drill the next five times. Hold your breath. Dig out the flesh with the Paper Mate, blot with toilet paper, exhale, and repeat. One continuous stroke, a circle, much quicker and cleaner than nearly every letter he'll need, except the "C." That one will be a present; he may even finish it off along with the letter G, which ain't nothing but a C with a fancy tail.

And that's how my Daddy's tattooed two-word prayer, and Good Luck," came to be.

"They can boo me and boot me out, but there ain't no one gonna get Jimmy Piersall out of Fenway. I'm forever."

He's swinging his imaginary golf club on the strip of lawn between our houses. I guess he's talking to me. I don't see anyone else nearby.

"Take a picture, Marlene," he says. "It'll last longer."

With the snarl of a feisty five-year old who does not mean it, I tell him, "Mom says a lot of people are mad at you. You disrespect Teddy Baseball even. I need my babysitting money. Please don't get traded." He walks over and tousles my hair. "Don't matter if I do, hon."

I love how his grin gets his fine blue eyes twinkling. His thick, sandy hair, combed back into a perfect swan swoop, gleams with Brylcream. His hair is the only part of him that stays still. Otherwise he's all circling arms, kicking legs, sashaying hips, bobbing his head. A roller that cannot coast no matter what park he walks.

"Want to know where my signature is?"

"What did you sign?" I love to find out where the words are. "Inside your locker?"

"Nothing permanent about where a man puts his stuff. No. I'm in a cave. There's a riddle for you. Five bucks says you can't figure it out."

I don't think he knows Fenway as well as Mom does. If there's a cave there, she's been inside it.

"The belly of the Green Monster." Mom is certain. "No better seat at Fenway Park in the house." She shimmies her shoulders, leans back into her kitchen chair, and lays back her head as if she's a pin-up gal. Springing up, she cranks her head forward, and makes eyeglass frames out of her hands.

I see she's squinting. "Oh, *mommelah*, I've imagined it a zillion times. I am sitting on a hard metal folding chair, and I'm peering out of my own little viewing slot, and I am, God help me, taking in the view from inside the monster's belly, the scoreboard in the wacky leftfield wall! Just underneath the red and green lights at the bottom of the scoreboard. Only three people can sit in this dungeon, and I'm one of them today. I'm hot, miserably hot. I'm breathing in dust. It's too dim to make out the signatures on the walls. But each one is an authentic autograph from one of ours."

Next morning, Jimmy raps on our front door. "Hey, Missy, can you sit my girls tonight? Heck, what with the short notice and all, I'll pay you double!"

"Sure. I can come over right now, if you like, so you and your wife can finish dressing up and stuff."

"You're a peach. Follow me." I did. I didn't take me but ten seconds to brag about my discovery, and make claim for my five dollar reward. I knew where his words found permanency.

"I know where you left your signature," I say, and tell him.

"So you figured it out, eh? I cut my name with glass from a broken beer bottle on the floor of that wall. Other guys did it with pen, proper and right. Nah, that won't do for Jimmy Boy. I had been ejected—for the fifth time last season—again." Jimmy stops short, slams his imaginary glove, and then, his sunglasses, to the ground. The same moves I've seen him make on TV.

Then he makes like he's taking a shower, soaping up, laughing, shaking his hair.

Oh yeah, sent to the showers but never willing to stop playing, Jimmy heads for the belly of the beast. The Green Monster gobbles him up. No one even sees him get inside the scoreboard, reach down for a slice of glass, and scratch in

J-I-M-P-I-E-R-S-A-L-L

I was my Daddy's daughter, that's for sure. But was he ever his daughter's Daddy? He called me his yellow bird. Said I was his whole world. Announced this to my mom, when I was four years old, "Irene, our little Yellow Bird needs a whole new wardrobe. She and I are thinking yellow. Everything yellow, even the shoes. Want to come shopping with me and my girl?"

Daddy and I are halfway out the door.

"Joey," Mom says, "I haven't bleached the toilets yet. Sorry."

Daddy nods, grabs my hand. "We'll keep it simple, Mommy. Promise. Maybe only a half-dozen yellow dresses. That's it. Nothing else."

"Joe, for Chrissakes, she isn't going to kindergarten for a whole other year. Why schlepp her out today? She is four years old. Four."

"Exactly my point, Irene! And how wonderful that she already knows what she wants!"

And that was how I learned early on that I had Daddy in my pocket.

But not anymore. My old Daddy was nowhere to be had.

Running backwards, what I had back then was a Daddy who needed me. He was the only one I understood. This was not, I think, a good way to enter the world of men.

Still. Still, even now, all I really do is dig in deeper and pretend. Pretend that even Boston's Big Dig will have a happy ending.

# 6

## Great Pretender

All it takes is one late morning sun to turn our parlor into a theater. Our wallpaper roses whirl to life. Even the fake ivy leaves on that wall-paper climb higher. Down Daddy walks in.

I usher him to his seat, turn my hand into a swan, gliding in front of him. He sits, folds his hands. An invisible puppeteer pulls up Daddy's bobbing head, *et voila*, his double chin lifts right along with it.

Too bad the strings can't corset his fleshy pear body; lift it right along with his head. And so it whales. One big Daddy sag. A shlump. Beached on his turquoise Womb Chair, he's got on his old man under-shirt; it swims freely over his Bermuda shorts. His bare feet, pigeon-toed, hardly anchor him.

But whoever works his face muscles, or the Daddy who lives inside, paints on a great big fat grin. I bow twice. Daddy's holding the grin still, even though that *no-goodnik* (a useless fellow) puppeteer has lowered his chin.

Forget it. Let him droop. I'm going on. I shake my head twice, toss it back, and bring my tight fist, a microphone, to my mouth. I belt out, "Oh-oh yes I'm the Great Pretender, Pretending that I'm doing well, My need is such I pretend too much."

I stop. I wait. I am ready to deliver Daddy's favorite move: the shimmy down the rose-whirled broadloom for the payoff:

"Too real is this feeling of make believe. Too real when I feel what my heart can't conceal."

Daddy, suddenly beaming, applauds; I blow puckered fish kisses, and pretend to be actress Loretta Young, all swirl and swivel down a spiral staircase, squid ink spit curls plastered to her head.

I take my bow. "Thank you, sir, thank you. There'll be an encore performance this evening, if you wish."

He does not wish. He does not wish. He does not wish. Not this Daddy.

When he was well, he'd scream, "Encore! Encore!" That is how it was between us just two years ago, when I was a fourth grader. Now in sixth, I cannot get "The Great Pretender" out of my head. I sing it on the way to school, in the bath, or whisper it like a prayer while I'm in bed. Some nights, even now, I fall asleep with the slippery refrain still wet on my lips.

Here's what has not changed: I pretend plenty. It may have been the Platters' biggest hit, but it's my little anthem. There's more. I can even control the darkness, and make up a bright future for Daddy. One day, Up Daddy and Down Daddy will balance their seesaw life. One day, they will look at each other from opposite ends, and nod their heads. Of course, it's only right that Down Daddy hits the bottom first, and with that, brings Up Daddy up. Up Daddy motions; Down Daddy kicks off slowly. They balance in the middle; neither move for what feels like forever. Suddenly, real politely, Up Daddy makes a "you first," and Down Daddy gets off.

Second later, so does Up Daddy! I will feel happier than I've ever felt. They will walk in opposite directions, and I will scream, "Good riddance to both of you!"

Truth is, great pretenders run in the family.

Take my Aunt Norma, for instance. Daddy's sister strings up wet tea bags on a taut little dolls' clothesline to dry and reuses them twice. She quarters a hard-boiled egg, slices an apple in eighths, and pretends it's lunch for four. This past *Chanukkah,* I sat on her plastic-covered sofa, opened my gift, and pretended how much I liked the scratched View-Master 3-D viewer, with a couple of bent paper reels to feed it, wrapped inside a nice big box from Bloomingdale's.

At Chanukkah, Aunt Norma brought me used coloring books, all scribbled up. Along with paper doll books, minus a doll and two, a missing tabbed hairstyle, and at least two of her six outfits. All stacked neatly, tissue-wrapped and placed inside *fancy*, *schmancy* picture frame boxes. Last year, a pilled sweater, despite Aunt Norma's comb out on the front of it, filled a starched shirt box. She had taped the crummy box with gold foiled wrapping paper, inside and out. Another disguise, another pretense.

Year-round, Aunt Norma buys up old novels and then later recovers them in glossy maroon and white book covers, with letters standing thick and straight as kings, from Harvard. But that's how they are on Daddy's side of the family, cheapskates on the giving but never sparing on the packaging.

In love with surfaces, the Rosenfields are. Except my Daddy, who lives from the inside out.

When I got tired of watching the bent-up reels that came with Aunt Norma's View-Master, tired of Little Lulu of the Sunday funnies bopping boyfriend Tubbie on the head, or of Buffalo Bob tricking Clarabelle the Clown, I tossed them, and decided I liked it better empty.

I click away while my fake extended eyes take in white light. I wait, I watch. I am a camera that soaks up the light, and fills in the right Daddy. And that's how my View-Master Daddy turns in 3-D, came to be. I snap on Danny Thomas Daddy, who is like the one on TV, waving his hand up in the air, and pretending his children drive him nuts, and it's as if my real Daddy has taken over for the TV Daddy.

While Down Daddy pretends to watch TV one night, and I fiddle with my empty View-Master, I get inspired. With a click, snap, click and pause, I conjure up my old Daddy, Top-Dollar Joe, the best used car salesman in Boston. Next to me, Daddy snores softly, his head lowered by the invisible puppeteer again. Meanwhile, the Daddy in my View-Master holds my hand and walks me past the abandoned seesaw Up Daddy and Down Daddy rode.

I bet I have the strongest index finger in the neighborhood. What with writing and clicking, I got a giant callous covering my finger tip. Lying in bed, I circle my eye with my thumb and index finger, and click off a few air reels. I even click when I sleepwalk.

Laugh at me, but some nights I say this prayer: "Click, click, click. Quick, quick, quick." And just like that, my old Daddy comes into view, dressed as the comfortable Daddy I knew as a little girl. Even in his backwards boxers, he looks like a king, a Top Dollar Daddy.

Also consider my *Zaydeh*. A plumber in Worcester, he pretended to be a learned man who had come from a long line of Russian rabbis, not from ignorant Lithuanian horse thieves, like my Bubbeh. He was not Russian but Lithuanian. He was not the family of rabbis; it was my Bubbeh's. He even pretended to have saved all five rabbis from more than one pogrom.

That my Zaydeh pretended to devour my sandy mud pies or pretended that he cared which doll was named what, well, this did not make him a liar. He called me Ma-lutch-ka-lah, and said he loved me more than all my cousins, all noisy boys. But it was them he took fishing, them he bought ice cream for, them he showed his calendar girls, them he listened to Hopalong Cassidy with, huddled over his transistor.

I, his Mah-lutch-ka-la, stood alone. Hand on hip, peeling off paint from Bubbeh and Zaydeh's garage or beheading dandelions and buttercups. That I won spelling bees, had the brains of my father's side of the family after all ("*tank god*," he'd say), and declared myself a sentence-maker at age seven, made me feel plenty lovable.

"Sshh!" he'd say to the cousins. "Don't you see what she's doing? She's making for herself a book. Shut up. Show some respect. It's easier to build a bridge than a book."

I made plenty of sentences at *Bubbeh* and *Zaydeh's*, all right, but only because they filled me up. Made me less lonesome. Still, he was my *Zaydeh*, and me, his granddaughter, an equation I mistook for his love. Until Skippy.

# 7

# Nobody

Morris Goldstein, the family's greatest pretender, loved the family dog, Skippy.

Here is what came of that love.

When Mom was just a young girl, she got polio from swimming down at Platt's Pond and had to stay in the city hospital, stuck inside a phony lung, *Zaydeh* stood out-side and yelled at Skippy to come home. But Skippy was not about to leave Mom.

She says she heard only two sounds from her hospital bed: the soothing swoosh swoosh of the iron lung and the whimpery whimpers of her Skippy from the hospital steps. Mom says the nurses, the cook, the secretaries, even a doctor, brought Skippy scraps of liver and lamb, and threw a blanket across Skippy's favorite step, the top one closest to the main entrance of the hospital.

Even when it rained three days straight and passersby tried to shoo him away, Skippy would not budge. Before his vigil, Skippy gobbled up whatever treats were thrown at him. Not then. Then he sat backwards on the topmost step, eyes fixed on the entrance, hungry only for his mistress.

Two weeks later, when Mom was ready to leave the hospital and Skippy spotted her in her wheelchair, he rose from his post and came with her and her mama. Simple as that. Back home, *Zaydeh* was cooking up his Lye soap and waiting for Skippy.

I start my science report with this: "Soaps are made from fats and oils. But it's the fatty acids that make soap soapy."

Like any kid, I think I might just as easily become a scientist as a writer.

I read aloud from the *Encyclopedia Britannica*, which Daddy couldn't sell, and so we have a sample set. "Thus to extract the fatty acids from the fats and oils," says the author, "One must treat them with a strong alkali."

AL-KA-LIE?

"Lye," says Mom. Her hands wrapped around her, she's rubbing an imaginary shiver away. She hugs me tightly from behind my black, wrought-iron bridge chair, in front of my desk. Another chair, a blonde mahogany, broke when my Uncle Jim, Daddy's oldest brother, sat on it. I giggle as I remember my tubby Uncle toppling the chair, plopping down into the seat, and yelling "T-I-M-B-E-R!" as the chair collapsed under him.

Now there was a sweet-natured liar! In kindergarten, every Monday afternoon, I would go straight to my Uncle Jim and Aunt Florence's house, just three blocks from school, for the hour or so that Mom and Daddy had to be at their doctor's appointment.

Anyway, I didn't mind. Uncle Jim's wife had bum plumbing. Which meant they couldn't have kids of their own, and so they loved everyone else's in the family. Lucky for me! I couldn't wait to see Uncle Jim's big toothy grin when he greeted me at the front door of their humongous colonial.

Every Monday the same: "Yes? What can we do you for you little lady?"

"Who we gonna call today, Uncle Jim?"

"That's up to you, honey. Marilyn Monroe, maybe. I got her unlisted number, natch. Would you like me to get her on the phone for you? Would you like that?"

I wouldn't.

"How 'bout I ring up Ernie Borgnine? Just sold him some property a month ago. A bit of a bore I might add. So who will it be today, little girl?"

"Rocky! Rocky! Rocky!"

And, just after my squeals, we burst out into our little cheer of a song, the first I ever wrote, to the tune of "Figaro."

"Marciano! Graziano! Marciano! Graziano!"

Then we do the dance: cross our arms, hold hands, and rock from side to side, singing "Marciano! Graziano!" For me, Graziano, now the best middleweight boxer, easily topped Marciano, heavyweight champion of the world.

Uncle Jim's belly bounces as we do our dance. On account of I'm Jewish, I do not say the "S" word in front of family, and, much as I want to, I'm not allowed to believe in the S-man in the red suit and the neat-o beard whose belly comes to mind.

"You know, sweetheart, we ain't limited today. Hell, could ring Rocky Colavito. Got his unlisted number right here," he says, pointing and poking at the spot just underneath his eyeglasses, right where the top of his cheek bulges the most. He never goes straight for the temple. As opposed to temple as in synagogue. None of that for Uncle Jim, who says his religion is Boxing.

Even though I adore the rhyming Rockies, I only want to stick with one of them. Both are very polite to me on the phone, and always say they love me before they hang up.

"WHO is Rocky Vito?" I ask.

"Oh God. Doesn't your Mama teach you anything but Red Sox? Rocky CO-LA-vito. Also known as The Rock. Aha! Plays for the Cleveland Indians."

But I already had plenty of baseball. Besides, I had begun to suspect that even the Red Sox were good at pretending, too. After all, Fenway Park could turn a good hitter into a batting champ. Even not so great hitters hit great at Fenway Park. All on account of the Green Monster; a left field wall built just a few feet closer to home plate. Course, I don't hear anyone admit it's a heck of a lot easier there to hit a ball that'll reach the fence. Nope, the great pretenders just pretend Fenway's like every other ballpark, and hit away!

Which is why I couldn't get enough of boxing. I didn't think boxers fooled themselves.

"Gravely Graziano, please."

"You sure? Cuz we could just as easily zip into my Caddie and have you meet the Brockton Blockbuster face to face. Five, ten minute drive, tops. Just say the word, little lady," and with that, he pinches my checks until they're pink. An Uncle Jim pinch makes the prettiest rouge.

"No, I want to talk to Graziano today. Definitely. He really, really is my favorite Rocky."

It would be almost ten years until I found out how Uncle Jim produced the rhyming Rockys for me. He'd put me in his real estate home office, just off his bedroom, sit me by the phone, close the door, and tell me not to pick up the extension until he shouted, "Hi-Ho Silver." Meanwhile, in another room, usually one of the three unborn babies' bedrooms, Uncle Jim would depress the receiver button, yell Hi-yo, Silver, and put on the gravely voice of Rocky Graziano.

Not until the summer of 1956, would I learn that Uncle Jim, ventriloquist, threw his pretend voice at me. Mom's only brother, my Uncle Mucko, had taken me and his son to see the new picture about the life of Rocky Graziano, "Somebody Up There Likes Me," starring the hunky Paul Newman. Uncle Jim had had a heart attack just two years before, and had dropped dead while driving his newest Caddie, a lipstick red. He had stopped for a red light and Pow! Right in the kisser, just like that, he made his last stop.

"So that's what he looked like!" I say to Uncle Mucko as we get up from our plush red velvet movie theater seats. "I spoke to the guy a zillion times. He was close friends with my Uncle Jim. Course I was just in kindergarten. Don't know how interesting I could've been to talk to, but every Monday."

"If your Uncle Jim had no balls, he'd be your aunt! Ha, ha, ha. Well, what am I saying? Your Uncle Jim had balls of brass. What a cut-up. Oh, and hey, he loved your Daddy. His baby brother Joey, he called him, even when they were grown men."

I'm humming "Marciano, Graziano," over and over, and rocking my head from side to side. Without my great pretender of an uncle, who would I have now to take me away from, well, me? In the front seat of Uncle Mucko's '55 Bonnet Blue Merc, my cousin tells my Uncle that, from now on, he's going to spit in public, just like Rocky Graziano. I've got my own song. In my head, all I hear is:

*Oh-oh, yes I'm the great pretender*
*Just laughin' and gay like a clown*
*I seem to be what I'm not, you see*
*I'm wearing my heart like a crown*
*Pretending that you're still around.*

A sentence maker learns to play ball from fat bats of books, encyclopedias, and dictionaries. Today I'm warming up at end of the Ls.

"Lye: an extreme caustic. Sodium hydroxide or potassium hydroxide cleans by a chemical reaction that burns or eats away other substances. Lye, also known as caustic potash, is commonly used in drain cleaner."

Its chemical action eats away materials (including skin tissue). Contact with skin or mucous membranes causes burns and frequently deep ulcerations with scarring. Eye contact causes severe damage, including blindness.

"*Mommelah*," says Mom. "Come, take a break from the paper. Sit with your old lady." She rips across her cigarette package, frisking the hidden side for another Lucky Strike.

"You've already got one lit, mom." I point to the traitor in the ashtray.

"You want to know about lye? Talk to me. I'm an expert."

"Cause Zaydeh used so much of it for his plumbing jobs?"

She nods her head. "Yeah, that, too." Her eyes narrow, her lips pucker, as she leans into her first drag. "I don't know what I should and shouldn't say. Maternal father. Huh! That would be an oxymoron."

"A what kind of moron?"

"Just means he wasn't much of a father." So she got short-changed, too.

"But he sure knew his poisons. My mama had nothing, really, poor immigrants, they scrimped for every dime, your Zaydeh even made his own soap. With lye."

"Wow! I'm putting this in my report."

"I don't think so, honey." She shakes her head. "I don't think so."

"Ivory soap he didn't make. If a raw egg sunk in your soap mixture, then you added more lye until the egg would rise to the top. One time, he poured enough lye into it to float a dozen eggs! He cooked it up special."

"For a really big plumbing job?"

She doesn't answer. "Ma, for what?"

"Not for what. For whom." Her eyes well up.

"Did he make you take a bath with it? Did he burn you with it? What, Ma, what?"

"No, not me. He made it up special for Skippy. The day I came home from the hospital, after my polio, and Zaydeh was out to get him."

"Out to get Skippy? This is crazy, Ma. Why would he want to hurt your dog, your best buddy?" She wipes her runny nose with the pot holder for my ceramic pin-making kiln.

"Skippy chose me. That's why. He stayed with me night and day at that hospital. And that son of a bitch, God forgive me, he hated him for it."

I wish I could smoke a gazillion cigarettes.

"The homecoming. Yeah. That's when I noticed the brew simmering on the stove. That was no goddamn chicken soup, that's for sure." She laughs. Then lets out a gigantic Oy. "What are you gonna do with the soap, Pa?" I ask him.

"Shampoo Skippy. Goddamn mutt stinks. Slept in rain, filthy rain. On the dirty stairs of hospital. God knows what he brought home with him. Once the soap cools down, I'll give him a decent scrubbing."

Mom heaves her head back, then shakes it. "Sweetheart, Zaydeh may as well have just set him on fire. Skippy is in the tub, barking a crazy high-pitched bark like you never heard. But, before I know it, Skippy wrestles out from under from Zaydeh's grip, jumps out of the tub, and hightails it to the street. Skippy, he is crying like a human baby, and he is rolling all over the middle of the road, rolling, rolling, and rolling to put out the fire under his fur. Maybe two, three minutes later, he's hit by a car."

"But you told me he got hit by a car like it was an *accident* accident." I am crying now, too. "That's all you ever told me, Ma. Why didn't you tell me you the truth?"

"Told you your Zaydeh hated the dog for loving me? No, this I could not say. To myself, even."

I had asked once if Zaydeh had ever hit my Bubbeh. A neighbor of theirs had called him a street angel and a house devil. Had he ever hit my Mom? She said he hadn't.

No, he had only killed her dog.

Once, I had seen Zaydeh slap Skippy. His eyes were wild with rage. Skippy whimpered, then wagged his tail, and curled up next to Zaydeh's easy chair. Zaydeh smiled, nodded his head, called him, "Good boy, good boy. You don't make Pa mad no more, right? Good. Now don't move. Lay with Pa."

I watched this Great Pretender pat his dog, and I knew. Right under the marriage *chuppah*, this *meshugenah* (crazy) grandpa had switched places with my real one. Bubbeh got the fake husband; Mom, the fake Daddy; and me, the Great Pretender song.

Oh yes, I'm the Great Pretender. Pretending That You're Still around. My needs are such, I pretend too much.

# 8

# What Happens to
# a Rosenfield

Crazy came in many voices, some barely audible, and it was to those crazies, the whispering crazies, that my second-grade teacher, Miss White, belonged. A wrinkly lady, with wisps of yellowing gray hair, she did not abide bad habits. And I had two of them: flirting with a boy and giggling with Anna Garabedian.

Miss White says if I keep "it" up I'll get the treatment. Only she makes the word sound like "treat men," and that makes me giggle even harder.

"Come with me, young lady," says Miss White. "Head toward the art supply storage room."

I march. I know what's waiting for me.

"Class, we know what this girl's problem is, don't we? And we know how to fix it, don't we? Observe." In a minute or two, she will place her hands firmly on my shoulders and begin her famous treatment. The Shake-up Treatment. Shaking me back and forth, back and forth, she will repeat my last name in combination with the same two words, "Out, out damn Rosenfield. Out, out, damn Rosenfield." Just twice. Just like that. Two shakes and I am done.

But, as I head back toward my desk, head down, she burst out with another lesson. I do not expect this, especially since someone's shake-up treatment is always followed by a minute of silence. What my classmates and me hear is this: "Ladies and gentlemen, you have just seen what happens to a Rosenfield."

Mom sighs, "You asked. So here goes." Stubbing out her Lucky Strike, she spreads her arms, makes cups of her two empty palms, then drops them to her lap. "Coffee stinks here. But what else can I wash this hot fudge sundae down with?"

We love to sit on the warm, red Naugahyde bench seats at Cabot's Ice Cream in Newton. Their leather may be fake, but the cherries on the sundaes are for real. Mom picks me up from Hebrew School every other week, and takes me out for a treat here. I may not make it to my Bat Mitzvah next November, but I will eat these sundaes with Mom as long as she's game. Another fifty years at least!

"My *tush* always sticks to these phony, naughty-hide seats. Which reminds me of another miserable seat, that itchy wool blanket at Old Orchard Beach in Maine, the fall of my eighteenth birthday. Your Zaydeh had put me on the bus, maybe the only nice thing he'd done for me, and ten hours later, I'm all by my lonesome. I'd been sitting on that miserable blanket, listening to my ballgame on the transistor, and booing at the ump. Someone asks me the score."

"Daddy?"

"What struck me was his confidence. Knelt down next to me and took over. I shut the radio off then and there. His first words? 'If you lost lost, say, twenty-five pounds, I'd marry you.' Introduces himself. This Joe Rosenfield had chutzpah in spades."

"And what makes you think this broad would marry you? Frankly, I'm holding out for someone with a little more hair. And maybe a little less beak, too. Come back after you've bought yourself a nice toupee, and we'll see."

"We'll just see who wants to marry who is what your old lady said."

"'WHOM. It's marry whom, Red. I'm a stickler for proper grammar,' says the dapper Mr. Rosenfield. 'I'm afraid I'm stuck with this honker. It's a Rosenfield family trait. And ix-nay on the toupee. We all got the cab-forward foreheads, a baldin' noggin. What you sees, lady, is what you gets.' Then he bows! Corny, yeah. But also charming."

"'Ditto,' I told him. I'm frisking my ugly blanket for a book of matches; got an unlit cigarette teetering on my lower lip. 'So take a good look, Rosenfield. Take your time.'

"Need a match, beautiful?" asks Joe.

"I haven't had a match since Gretta Garbo," I said. "That cracked him up."

"'I see I've got a live one here. A flame for my soon-to-be flame,' and with that, he lights my cigarette." As if Daddy's next to our booth this very moment, Mom pops another ciggie in her mouth and looks around. When the waitress asks if she can refresh her coffee, Mom says, no, thanks, but I do need a light.

My parents met one frigid Labor Day at Old Orchard Beach in Maine of 1935. Only three months later, three scrawny months later, my Daddy's dropping hints. Like this: dress real nice for dinner, Irene. We'll be stepping out someplace fine. That night he takes her to dinner at The Copley, Boston's ritziest, oldest hotel.

And this: when she opens her menu, Daddy gives it a gentle tug, slaps it on the table, and tells her, go ahead, order the lobster, Mom knows something's up. That a poor *schlepp* (low brow) from Worcester, Mass should eat *traif* (non-kosher) is one thing; that she eats it at Boston's Copley Hotel practically makes the shellfish kosher.

Along with my Daddy's marriage proposal there, at the Copley, on Mom's Armistice Day birthday—on my favorite set of numbers, Eleven Eleven—comes something from his pocket. It is not a ring box. No. What he pulled from his trousers' pocket was a bracelet. Just like that, he removed her knife from her place setting, and replaced it with his gift. Once Daddy had stretched it alongside her dinner plate, Mom spotted the clock's face in the middle of the bracelet. What she said was:

"Nu? A gold watch. Am I retiring, Joey?"

"I'd say so, Renee," Daddy quipped. He has not used this pet name for his redheaded Irene before.

Mom unclasps her watch, wriggles out of it, and reaches for my wrist. She says it'll be mine someday, so why not now? Why not? Because I'm still her little *pisher* (little kid), even if I've just had my 20th birthday. Because the watch is too expensive, too elegant, too gold, too, well, gaudy for a girl who wears a Timex.

Truth is, the watch comes to me with too much time on it; more time than I want to track. It's hard for me to look at the watch too closely, as if the glare off the crystal might be harmful to my vision. In my mind's eye, I imagine it through Mom's eyes.

This is what I see. Mom eyes the rubies and diamonds that surround the watch face, the hefty gold bars linking the vertical Vees, just like sets of parenthesis. Even in the dimly lit dining room of the Copley, the rubies flash like emergency lights off, on, off, on. The fire of the diamonds trips off an alarm inside her belly. She felt a rumble, wonders if the lobster may have poisoned her. Then a second pang in the pit.

"Turn it over," my Daddy commands. "Go ahead, Irene. Please. Read the inscription. I had them do it in all caps, so you can still read it fifty years from now. I think ahead."

Aloud, Mom reads, "Marry me. Joe to Irene. 11/11/35."

This imperative, this command, had come less than seven weeks after a courtship of three dates. Since they lived forty miles apart, three times my Daddy will have driven three successive Sunday afternoons to see her. A couple of love letters. Plus two phone calls.

Daddy springs from his plush purple velvet seat at the Copley, scoops up the bracelet watch, and takes Irene's hand with his free one. "You taking my pulse now, Joey? I'm feeling a little faint. Probably a good idea."

"Yes, I'm saying yes, I'll take your pulse, right along with the extra twenty-five pounds that come with it. I expect I'll be bald by New Year's, so I was hoping for a December wedding." He fastens the clasp on her wrist. "What a beauty. The watch ain't half bad either."

Irene can't take her eyes off the emergency on her wrist, the rubies still flashing, the diamonds still firing. Light, light, God Bless your eyesight.

Joe adds, "My jeweler and I have been staying up nights for almost a month, working on this baby. The design is all mine. It's been in my head for ages."

# 9

# Speeding Home to Mama

As my Mom tells it, after the engagement dinner, Daddy sped home. To his mama's home, a brick, four-bedroom Tudor in Jamaica Plains, Massachusetts, where the smart, rich Jews live.

Mom had grown up in a coldwater flat, where my Bubbeh used to heat a bunch of bricks, wrap them in a towel, and put them in her daughter's bed to keep her warm. ("Here, *meine kinde*, take a prick in your bed," Bubbeh would say, who often mixed up the letters "b" and "p.") This from my Mom.

Anyway, that night, a very happy Joe Rosenfield yells, "Ma, Ma," as he bangs on his mother's front door. "Quick, Ma, open up." (The key was in hand, but Daddy always preferred urgency.)

His mother looks out at the couple, nods her head, and waves them into the narrow vestibule behind her. Her back is already turned, as she makes a beeline straight down the hall. Joe walks behind her and behind him, Irene.

"Well," says Joe's mother, "What was all that commotion?"

Joe is beaming. He steps behind, grabs behind him for Irene's hand, and pulls her forward with a slight jerk. "Ma," he says, "I'd like you to meet the next Mrs. Rosenfield. Ta-da!" His mother's lips pucker. Shaking her head, she moves the teakettle from the stove to the sink. The water gushes out in one fat stream.

"The next Mrs. Rosenfield? Really? The next Mrs. Rosenfield? Shame on you, Joseph! Your father had far better taste."

Who would try to keep a surprise on a schedule? Last Wednesday came with a hot fudge sundae, and two scoops of surprise! How my mom became a Rosenfield. Which leads to surprise number two: she got herself one husband she barely knew, and another she wouldn't meet for years. Voila: this little Rosenfield wound up with two Joe Rosenfields, all wrapped into one.

Since this is a Wednesday without a sundae (ha ha), I have time to skip rope with the girls after Hebrew School. Another surprise: An older kid who wouldn't talk to us is now saying she'll teach us this name game. Just like that. Starting from "A," she tells us, you make up wives, husbands, places to lives, even jobs. Who knows from men with "E" names—not me. Out. Bye-bye.

Wouldn't you know it? Riding the bus home, I come up with Elijah and Elias, who is the same Hebrew prophet, I think. Can't keep any of those *meshugenah* (crazy) prophets apart. All of them angry; all dreamers and drama. Elijah. Who rode a chariot. I'll turn that into his job: "E my name is Ellen, my husband's name is Elijah, we live in Europe and we sell Edsels." There. A little practice tonight, and I'll be ready to roll through the alphabet on my own.

Soon as I get in the house, I know Mom's frying smelts. That means Daddy's not coming home. The baby bones get caught in his esophagus.

"Fee-fi-fo-fum, I smell the smelt of an Englishman," I say. Grinning, Mom grabs for a dish rag to wipe her hands, then crumples my chin and makes her lips into a big fish kiss. Smooch, smooch.

She points to the floury mess on wax paper. "I'll fry up that eggplant for Daddy later."

Eggplant, yeah! That's what Elijah-Elias can sell. Why stick him with an Edsel, a stupid joke of a car. Without a jump rope, I hop on my right leg and belt out: "'A' my name is Alice, my husband's name is Al, we come from Alaska, and we sell alfalfa," and let my left leg pick up the slack. Mom's already at the table, eating her smelts with her hands. She taps on my seat at the table. I gobble my smelts down two and three at a time.

"I see your Hebrew education has finally begun to pay off, honey."

"The Name Game, Ma! After dinner, you and I can play it without a jump rope."

"Good," she says, "Because I left mine in the office."

"You start with the letter A, and move up the alphabet. A my name is Alice, my husband's name is Al, we live in Alaska, and we sell aardvarks. Your turn, ma. You do B."

"I got a better idea, honey. How 'bout I tell you about the A, Alley, I didn't marry? I'll be on the porch." She heads for the porch with ciggies and matches in hand.

Bye-bye to the letters B, C and D. I'm getting the scoop on Alley first.

# 10

# Alley, the Chicken Plucker

I hightail it to our scrawny, screened-in porch. Not even twice the size of our bathroom, the porch can only hold two people: me, on the floor, sitting on my *tush*, and Mom on her throne, a beat-up, bright green lawn chair woven between teeth-colored strips. Like rotting teeth, three of them dangle on the floor. Most days, I can't get to our little porch fast enough, can't hear enough of Mom's kooky stories. No bedtime stories, these. Stories so wide that you want to wrap yourself up in them, make of them a shawl. Please, pass the cigarettes!

How we love our ciggies, Mom and me.

What you hold between your fingers is power, is promise, and is prayer for a different way to be. A more mature, less gawky you, your best friend, your ciggies, will stand by you. Plus, this is America. Smoke as many as you want, whenever you want. You pays your money, and you gets your cigarettes.

Mom's stretches out on her limp lounger; iced coffee in one hand, a butt in the other. "Would you believe I jumped to the same song, Marlene-a-la? Jumped, too, for my Alley."

Second time she's dropped Alley on me. I snag her ciggies and light up, saying, "Continue, *s'il vous plait*." Me and my puffy cheeks (face and tush) plop down on the floor beside her.

I'd like to blow out my first drag in one long smoke ring, only I don't really know whether you have to suck it in first, or store it inside your checks.

"I wish you hadn't brought that jump rope song home. Brought Alley Rudner back into this house."

Foolishly thinking I could mix my second drag in with the smoke already in my mouth as I choke. And choke again.

"Sweetie, I can't afford to keep us both in smokes." She grinds hers out, and uses the stubby pencil butt to circle the ashtray with it. She traces the rim over and over. This means she's going to spill the beans but not until she's taken a great big swig of her iced coffee. The mug sits snuggly on a double green ceramic circle. The lip on one circle reads "Java"; the lip on the other circle reads "Jive." Perfect fit for a nice onion bagel with a *schmear*, this circle has becomes Mom's favorite ashtray. I nab the extra book of matches next to it, pull the first three matches forward, careful not to rip them, and start braiding them together. For ages and ages, I've been braiding matches to Mom's stories.

"Uh uh. I may need to braid them matches myself when I can't fall asleep. Or maybe I just borrow your jump rope and skip myself to sleep?" She shifts in her green-and-white plastic chaise lounger. Squeak, squeak. Sitting squat-style on the floorboards, I do a little *tush* walk (arms folded in front of me, push down on my right check, then my left), to get closer to the ashtray, and stake my claim in front of her feet. I pull off the third drag without as much as a peep.

I tell her I won't be smoking that much. Just mooch a few, here and there. "C'mon. You had a guy named Alley and what? He dumped you? Daddy was your first real love. Glad Alley dumped you so Daddy could pick you up."

"Freezing. Made my teeth chatter. Antarctica, otherwise known as Old Orchard Beach in Maine, where Zaydeh had sent me to get over Alley. It's there I met Joe."

Joe? That's all? Joe. A regular guy with a scrawny, three-letter name, not a lovey dovey name, like sweetheart or honey or sugar pie. Just Joe—as in just anybody. C'mon. How come she does not call him Top Dollar Joe? Even way back then, my Daddy must've been a king, or at least a handsome prince. Why'd she go and steal his title, Top Dollar Joe, and turn him back into an ordinary guy, a "Regular Joe"?

"Zaydeh put me on the bus. Must have figured it'd cost him less than a trip to the sanatorium. Funny, that's the only thing Pa ever did for me. Course, it ended up a very big thing, a marriage. Hey, hey, hey, little pisher! Speaking of big stuff, anyone ever tell you you're too young to smoke?"

"Why did Alley dump you?" I ask, and, still nauseated, light my second cigarette.

"I'd had a bad break, a heart break, couldn't get out of bed. Missed 3 days work. So Pa ordered me to spend the weekend on the beach, and there I sat, oozing and shvitzing out Alley, the love of my life. And the best chicken plucker Mitzy ever had."

I eye the cigarette carton on the folding table, pull it toward me and count eight packs.

Grinning and cocking my head, I fix on the carton. Then I tell her, "Ma, you have a hundred and sixty cigarettes left." I can't hold back the giggle. "You're kidding, Ma, right? A chicken plucker?"

She inhales deeply, exhales, and her face starts to redden. "And why not, you little pisher. What do you know from plucking? Alley made better money than my old man. Three cents a chicken. Five chickens an hour. Three, four hours every day after school. Nu? What's that add up to, Miss Mathematics?" She rises, faces the front of the screened-in porch, and smooths out the dimples in the screen.

"Ma, I stink in math."

"C'mon, let's get off our fat *tushes*. We're out of toilet paper," she says, frisking her patch pockets for a light.

I love the way Mom's eyes narrow as she takes her first drag. I'm copying that! Such a kool kat look. Also, I plan to be very nice at the grocery so I can wrangle my own pack out of her. Fat chance.

The next afternoon, I have to make-up a stupid French test, which makes me late for supper. Taking the stairs two by two, I smell cooked carrots from the hallway. It's the first dinnery dinner we've had in a while. Me, I love what I call a Backwards Dinner: a scoop of ice cream, a glop of Hershey's syrup, a cherry on top. Maybe an hour later, an egg salad sandwich. But it's not the dinner I'm rushing toward. It's having my fourth cigarette in less than an hour, well, that makes my mouth water, making me feel more adult, less like Daddy's yellow bird. Smoking makes everything look brighter.

I can't just walk into the kitchen and bum a cigarette. What I say instead is, "Mom, I got a hundred on my test." Whenever she finally sees me, she cocks her head to the right, grins as wide and as bright as the 160 chrome squares on the '58 Buick that outshone all the other chrome grille work in Top Dollar Joe's lot. When she smiles, Mom's eyes shine like the big "cat's eye" tailgates on the two-toned lemon-and-lime Studebaker always parked next to that Buick. Her eyes, like her eyebrows, are two different colors, the red eye brow sits atop the hazel green eye; the blonde one arches over the brown eye. Nothing about my mother is a repeat.

"Sweetheart," she says, saddling over to me and holding her puckered up lips to mine, "What a delicious combination. Your kiss and my brisket! Yup. Mitzy gave me—on credit—three pounds of ground chuck, two roasters, and a tongue, too." She sticks out her tongue; it's what my family always does when either of us even mentions tongue. Ha ha.

Mitzy, of Mitzy's Meats, is the last kosher butcher to stay open in a city that once had three of them. I don't care if my meat is kosher, and neither do half the Jews in the country.

"Ma, how will you pay Mitzy?"

"I'll have Daddy's last commission check then, that's how." She bows her head and does an about face, heading again for her chaise lounge. I frisk the pocket on her housedress for her cigarette pack. She stops my hand with hers. "Buy your own, little Miss Grubber, if you please. C'mon, *meine kinde*, let's eat early. Daddy's not coming home to eat tonight."

After dinner, I rinse the dishes and sing, "A tasket, a tisket, how I love mom's brisket." I'm setting her up.

She breaks out into her cackle. When she catches her breath again, she smiles and says, "Kosher. Nu? Sit awhile. I haven't finished my coffee yet. By the way, you plan on drinking coffee now, too?

I nod.

"You know what I once saw in the paper? By the *goyim*, everything's a contest. Even killing. Some *meshugannas* in Florida, veterans of foreign wars, *ich vaysht nit* (I know not) hold an annual chicken plucking contest. Year after year, they get together to see who could strip the most feathers of a steaming bird in 20 seconds."

Good one! She will prove why Jews are kinder to their kill, and find her way back to the best chicken plucker of them all. "Ritual slaughter, Ma? Ritual slaughter is an oxymoron."

"A what kind of moron?" she asks, pretending not to know the word.

"Ma, there's nothing nice about slaughter. Period."

"That depends on who is doing it, doesn't it?" she says, a Lucky Strike bouncing between her lips, as she fumbles to light up in victory. "Hundreds of caged chickens under a tent until the crazy bastards—who call themselves 'handlers'—open the cages, grab them by the neck, swing them around, and strangle them. Go figure."

I'm thinking Mom has outdone herself. I count three distinct morals: One: you'd never find a Friedman Chicken in a cage; they shuffle along freely on his farm, which is as close to a cushy life at Grossinger's resort as a chicken can get. Who knows? Maybe Friedman's chickens even retire to suites at night. Waking up, they head for a big breakfast before they themselves are dinner. Two: Jewish law says *tzar baalei chaim*—any cruel treatment—is a no-no. Turning chickens into lassoes speaks for itself. Three: Alley the chicken plucker, and all the great Jewish chicken pluckers who came before and after, would not stoop so low as to pluck a live chicken.

Strike the first two morals. Alley lives inside every chicken. He's even inside the three dead ones in our fridge. "So who kills Mitzy's chickens these days?"

"Oh mommelah, how you bring me back! You didn't know Mitzy's big brother, Harry, may he rest in peace. Alley's boss. Harry was a *schochet*. His blade made quick work of it one quick stroke cut across the chicken's windpipe, the carotid arteries, and the jugular vein. The goyim drag the chicken's heads and necks through water. I read that some *schmendrick* figured out how to put electricity into that poisonous water."

"Enough, Ma. Really. Too yucky. Let's get off this stupid subject." I mooch Mom's butts and pull hard on the first drag. Ouch! Why should my throat still burn after all these months?

"Let me tell you how my Alley worked with his hands. He was a magician with his hands," she says, sighs loudly, shakes her head, and draws the smoke in, and exhales with another sigh.

What men do with their hands—particularly their gloved hands — that's what matters the most to Mom. Men like Jimmy Piersall, her number one hero. Him, plus the entire Boston Red Sox. The men who catch the balls, the ones who throw them, the ones who pitch them, these are the men of my mother's fantasy life.

Once she had said to me, "And they say Jews aren't good with their hands. Bullshit. Have these schnooks seen the likes of a Sandy Koufax?"

"Of all Harry's pluckers, Alley was the fastest, his birds the cleanest. You'd need magnifying glasses to find a pinfeather on his chickens. Alley had huge calluses on his thumbs and index fingers, but when he touched me—well enough." In the ashtray, I see the three neat little rows of ashes she has made are about to be slain. She turns the cover of her matchbook into a spatula, and with one swift scoop, she upturns her tidy rows.

All of a sudden she snuffs out her half-smoked cigarette, a signal she's going to bed early. I don't want to let her go to the places she'll wander while she's falling off to sleep. Alley lurks in the corners, and maybe other men, too, men who can hurt worse than Daddy.

I try to talk her into a little TV.

Too late. As soon as she turns around, says "No, thanks," I see her nose has started to run. "Quick, *meine kinde*," she says. "Help me. Kleenex." I can get her a tissue. But help her? No. This I cannot do.

It makes me crazy, how you can love someone and they can love someone and still…still you can't get your love swinging in the right direction, and finally, finally like the great Ted Williams, ad d cork to that swing, and unleash the monster ball once and for all.

The next week, I decide to cut Wednesday Hebrew School, and take the bus instead to Mitzy's. One customer inside, and who is it? Just my luck, it's my Uncle Mucko, mom's only brother, inside. Mitzy has just passed him his order.

"Hey, kiddo!" he says when he sees me. With Mucko, it's always kid or kiddo, never Marlene. Wait. I think he even calls his wife and kids kiddos.

"What are you doing over this part of town? Take the wrong bus from school?" He tousles my hair, and with his free arm, rings me close to him.

"I came here to thank Mitzy. He gave mom credit." There. That sounds like a good reason. Better than saying I am here to get the dirt on Alley.

Annoyed, Mucko shouts at Mitzy. "What? Mitzy, you schmuck, put Irene's meat on my tab. Don't you take a dime from Irene. You hear me?"

"Yeah, sure, big man," says Mitzy.

"Mucko, Mucko, just who you callin' a schmuck?" shouts Mucko. "You're calling me, me your schmucko? It don't rhyme with Mitzy. Nah, that honor's reserved for Ditzy." Mitzy and Mucko go way back. Fought in the same platoon. Despite that, Mitzy sounds as angry at Mucko as he does at any customer, his answers are clipped like curses.

"You want a ride home, kiddo?" I had come to Mitzy's to get the goods on Alley. I wasn't leaving. Much as I love riding in his Cadillac. He calls it his Jew Canoe. Funny how Jews can get away with that stuff, make fun of themselves with other Jews. I don't know how.

"No, thanks," I say, "But Uncle Mucko? I'm wondering about Alley, Mom's Alley. For instance, what kind of baby name is that for a grown man to have? Is it Allan, or something finky like Albert?"

"What the hell's wrong with the name? It stands for Elias," Mucko explains. "It's the guy who ain't no good, right, Mitzy? Imagine that schmuck named after a Hebrew prophet? Elijah no less. A sacrilege."

Everyone's either a schmuck or a kiddo.

And that's how my Uncle Mucko, a golfer, slices the world in two.

Just me and Mitzy left now. Good. No more customers to get in the way of me and Alley. He puts up the closed sign in the window of his butcher shop. Even better!

He gives me little suspicious look. "What'cha want to talk about Alley for anyway?" He pulls a Camel from his pack.

I open my purse and pull out a Marlboro. I had scored three at recess.

"When did you take up smoking, you little bum!"

Last week, I tell him. "It's kind of something neat to do with my mom." I sound like I'm five years old again, excited about making Popsicle stick houses, instead of sharing cancer sticks.

"Great. Glad to see it," says Mitzy, and knuckles me playfully on the head. "So what's with all the questions on Al? You writing a book?"

"Maybe" is what I say, and since he doesn't answer, I figure I ought to say more. "Just maybe I will end up a famous novelist."

"If you live past eighteen. You still getting straight A's? You still kissing your books up and down their spines when you're done reading them?" His face softens with affection for me and for his own love for books. He's always got a book open on his butcher block; one hand cuts the meat; the other flips the pages. Mom borrowed the great I. B. Singer from him, and showed me a few the blood-stained fingerprints where Mitzy turned the pages. I figure Singer would be flattered.

"I just discovered the best writer in the whole world. Arthur Miller. Read *Death of a Salesman* for English. I felt so grateful to Arthur Miller for this play that I almost kissed his beautiful punim right off the book jacket."

He says "I prefer his bride—Miss Marilyn Monroe—to the ugly mug on that bald guy with the specs. You're a funny girl, you are. Grateful? What is it you owe Arthur Miller? You borrowed a few bucks from him, maybe?"

"Nah, I just love Arthur Miller is all. Great character, Willy Loman. Our English teacher says he stands for Everyman." What I don't do is recite all the dialogue I've memorized, or get schmaltzy and say what I believe to be true, that Willy is no Everyman; Joe Rosenfield is.

Before I knew it, I would soon have proof. I will have seen Daddy act more like Willy Loman than Willy Loman ever did. One sunny Monday morning, I will walk into the kitchen and see my Daddy standing with his back against our sweet pink Frigidaire refrigerator. My mother and he will be standing face to face. Me, I will feel like I was Arthur Miller, holding a glass to our kitchen wall, eavesdropping on Down Daddy's crying jag.

"God, Irene, they're not even calling me back, "says Down Daddy, "And when no one even smiles at you anymore, you're finished, kaput. If I'm not a salesman, I'm dreck." "Dreck," he repeats, then flips his head backward, banging it on the fridge twice, adding a pounding period to each of his drecks. Right along with Willy's wife, I deliver Miller's final blow, and mouth my favorite lines, "When they start not smiling back that's your earthquake."

Mitzy cleans off his bloody cleaver. "You're ready to close. I wondered, could I ask you a few questions. For a term paper on kosher slaughtering," I lie. "I won't put in stuff about how Harry did things." Lie number two. "Would now be okay?"

Off comes his bloody apron. "Now is all any of us get."

Good. I'm in like Flynn.

"Fire away." He tips his cap, removes it. "Here, come let's sit." He motions to the bridge chairs lined up in front his back freezer case. "Welcome to my parlor," he says, then takes a plastic wrapped cigar from his shirt packet, bites off the end, spits it on the sawdust floor, and puffs away. I wish he'd offer me one. "I'll tell you from Harry, gentle soul, may he rest in peace. You know, when he retired, I had an awful time with other *shochets* (kosher butchers).

What's the matter with Harry's replacement? Does he check the knife for nicks?' she asked me. Yup, I told her. 'Does he drain the blood quickly and check the lungs?' I nodded again. So, tell me, darling, what is the problem with the new shochet?"

Mitzy shakes his head and snickers.

"I told my wife that the new guy didn't do the one thing that made my Harry, God rest his soul, impossible to replace: Harry used to cry afterwards. He felt for those chickens. Every day came another cry from my brother." Mitzy relights his cigar. "You don't find such a loving soul, such a shochet like that, in a lifetime, now do you?"

Since I know all about lifetimes, all about Daddies Down and Up, what I say is, "No."

"That Harry was not bloodthirsty, that he suffered along with what he slaughtered, well, that's what made Harry irreplaceable."

I love the smell of Mitzy's cigar.

"Soon, there'll be machines to do all this. Automatic neck cutters for the chickens. I already hear talk about de-feathering machines. Christ almighty." Mitzy groans.

"Gee, I guess guys like Alley wouldn't have had a job if there were machines back then. No more plucking by hand," I say.

"Alley? What the hell makes you bring up that no-goodnik?" says Mitzy. Big grimace. "Your mama used to run here every day after school, and sit here for three, four hours, just watching Alley pluck. Poor girl, she'd leave covered in feathers every darn day, and she'd come back the next, feathers still stuck to her shoes."

"Course, we were, all of us, just kids back then. Fourteen, fifteen years old, maybe. I don't think your Mama missed a day. Just sat on a stool next to Alley. And for what? Pardon my French, but he *shtupped* Irene good."

I'm smart enough to know Mitzy is not talking about *sex*, sex.

"Again, pardon my French, but you can *shtupp* (*screw over*) a girl lots of ways." Mitzy takes me back to my Bubbeh and Zaydeh's tenement house on our single-street Jewish ghetto, Water Street, right across the street from our shul. "Us kids, me, your Uncle Mucko, his cousins Schmull and Miltie, we would shoot marbles before Hebrew school some days, and maybe a little stick ball after." Mitzy turns to me. "You want maybe a soda pop?"

I shake my head. "Thanks, anyway." What I really want to say is I'd rather try your cigar.

"Anyway, one day, your Uncle Mucko and me seen a limousine with New York plates been parked just around the corner. Knew something was up. In a neighborhood like ours, you don't see limos. I inquire, I find out Alley came up from the big city the night before. He had been tripping the light fantastic with more than his aging *tantah* and auntie's fancy schmancy quarters. Upper West Side no less."

Mitzy pauses, spits out anger along with cigar. "Aaach. What can I say? Alley, the *goniff* (thief), was inside the shul that next morning. Waiting at the altar for his girl. And that girl was not your old lady."

After walking in on Alley's wedding-in-progress, my Uncle Mucko ran across the street to his house, let Bubbeh and Zaydeh in on the secret wedding. Zaydeh was standing up, eating from the *shabbos cholent* (Ch, like the Ch in Bach), and smacked Mucko on the head for not stopping the wedding.

Bubbeh kept shushing them, just like Alley did when he heard Mucko and Mitzy pull open the heavy brass door to the sanctuary. The sneak turned around, crossed his lips with his bloody index finger, and nodded. Then he plucked a pretend hair off his suit, and swiveled round to his old rich bride-to-be.

Was Alley stupid enough to have been hoping that his Irene, who'd always stayed up late listening to a Red Sox twilight double header, might just sleep through his nuptials? Or worse. That he didn't care.

Know what I would have done? I'd have plucked every hair off him. Plucked inside his nasty nostrils, beard, sideburns, head, shoulders, back, legs, arms, underarms, chest. Pluck, pluck you fuck.

Mom's motto, then and now, "You have got to get up pretty early in the morning to put one over on me," must have meant she hadn't slept through Alley's wedding.

No. Instead she listened in the dark to her beloved Red Sox. She heard them lose not one, but two, games and blow their four-game lead over the Yankees. Even now, Mom could never get herself to fall sleep after an upset like that. I imagine she had looked out her window, across from the shul, saw the limo waiting, and put one and one together. After all, on her tiny block, everyone knew who'd be getting married when.

For sure, Mom had watched the day break. Break apart. Swallowed up, too, was daylight for three days straight.

After my visit with Mitzy, I catch the last Hebrew school bus home and find Mom on her chaise, leaning over her ashtray, working her matchbook cover. She wedges the cover barely under her upside triangle of ash.

She turns to me and says, "I flip it; it falls apart. Mommelah, I hear you've been pretty busy yourself this afternoon." She retracts her matchbox cover, dices up the triangle of ash, and then parts it in half.

Mitzy, that *yenta*!

"Not really busy," I say, "not like you have," pointing toward the ashtray.

"My experiment was a flop! I thought I might be able to fashion a little heart for myself out of the ashes. But I had no way to round out the edges. Not with my tools," she says, then grins, and repeats, "not with my tools. What would you say about these two words together: whole heart. Would they make a moron—or an oxymoron?"

Tearing up, her one brown eye and one green eye look exactly the same.

"All that detective work and you know nothing? Listen to me, meine kinde, Alley—Elijah Howard Rudner—is the love of my life." Stabbing her cigarette into the ashtray three times, she says with each stab: "Is. Is. Is."

Some of what I found out about Alley later wasn't for telling. That he couldn't wait to get his fingers working a just-killed chicken; its skin still warm from the blood that had traversed it, then had been let out of it. Alley would spread its wings apart, hold it down to the ground with the heel of his right hand (he plucked with his left, making him singular still), and try to beat his last record-breaking pluck—eight minutes, including two for burning off the pinfeathers. He could not stave off rigor mortis every pluck, and it infuriated him.

What Mucko and Mitzy couldn't get out of their minds was one particular day a month before Alley's wedding. A day Alley had to grab hold of his stomach, because the sight of a chicken wobbling round and round, its muscles in spasm, its head cut off, brought on a laughing fit. Mucko did not want his sister married to this sadist, and, like any big brother, vowed then that he would do everything he could to save Irene from Alley.

Alley's wedding had saved him the trouble.

Alley Cat, Alley Cat, Big Fat Rat, what in the world made you do that? How could you behead my mother like your chickens? Did you imagine her writhe, wiggle, and wobble? You, Alley, are amazed at how quickly she gave in, how completely she out bled all over those other chickens, headless whores in your hands.

You rise, Alley, from the three-legged stool where you sat for three years, plucking, plucking, and plucking, preparing your calloused fingers for this kill (slaughter, slaughter, whoops there goes another Jewish daughter. daughter) and take your leave. You emerge from a limousine, squiggle, straighten out, and look up to my mother's bedroom window, then turn your back. You pull open the doors to the sanctuary, head straight for the most scared of places, the *bima*, of your *shul*, while Irene twitches in her sleep across the street.

These will be Irene's nightmares for most of her life. In the first, she is a baby suddenly, with dimpled skin turned slightly yellow, and that her skin starts to pucker all over. She doesn't have a hair on her head. Bald as baby.

In the second nightmare, Irene isn't just bald, but also very, very old, with the crinkly wrinkled skin of an old hen. Her arms, under arms, private parts, and legs: all hairless. Her skin tightens suddenly, as if it has been ironed smooth. Tentatively, she touches her smoothed skin, and screams. Instead of skin, she's covered in wax. Instead of arms, wings. Near her is a chariot. She's not sure whether to get in and ride it, or use her own wings and fly.

Last nightmare: Stuck up in the sky, Irene has awful *shpilkes*—so bad, in fact, she'd jump out of her skin were it not wax. She has got to find a cigarette to calm her down. What to do but fly and see if she can spot a pack below? So she tries out her wings for the first time, and like a yellow bird, flies a couple feet and nearly smacks into the charioteer, her Elijah.

"You need a match, honey pie? Yeah, yeah you haven't had a match since Marilyn Monroe. C'mon. You always let me light you up." Alley's chariot is on fire.

"Yes, please. A cigarette, too, if you can spare one."

"Ha, ha. You were always such a riot. But I can't help you out. I'm traveling in the opposite direction."

Elijah soars skyward with his chariot of fire.

Irene, of course, can't catch him. After all, he's a soul on fire. He can't change his direction. Irene picks up her speed, turns herself around. Tries to go up instead of down. Knows it is impossible to catch her Alley, that he will consume her even in their heaven.

So just like the Up Daddy she would come to know, she rises, not knowing, but sensing, Up might soon be Down—down, down, down, you never turn your luck around. You only fly this way once.

Soaring, soaring, heading straight for the fire, for the sun, Irene, like Icarus, knows she has made a huge mistake. She has flown too close to the flame; her wings and her feathers, both, melt. Her body separates at the neck, not human, but fowl. At least she's still got her head. Grounded for good, she will be forced to travel earth with another: another who is down, flying far too low to the ground.

But for now all she wants to do is wake from the nightmares, go home, swap her chicken neck, and offer it to her mama who will add it to her soup. Bones, chicken bones, from the feet, from the neck, are the secret of my Bubbeh's sweet broth. When she doles out the soup on *shabbos*, she still puts the chicken neck in her daughter's bowl. In Bubbeh's bowl? Chicken feet. She'd suck the marrow. Natch, we all thought Bubbeh loved those feet. She was just pretending, too. She ate the feet so there'd be enough chicken in the soup to feed Zaydeh and their children.

# 11

# Pinned

If I'm at Bubbeh's house, chances are I'm pinned to the kitchen chair. I won't be moving from her kitchen all day. And why would I? Sure, she makes plenty of weird stuff, but it always tastes *gaschmuckt*, (yum, yum, yum). Today she's shaving cow hooves and using the shavings for Zaydeh's favorite pudding, then peeling *ba-ta-tuhs*, and slicing carrots *mit* onions to plop in with the boiling chicken feet the butcher gives away.

Whenever I hear the sizzling of the onions blackening in the pan on Bubbeh's stove, I look up at the shiny oilcloth walls, and imagine the bright red-orange hens and roosters squawking and swapping tales. Lucky them, they see and hear it all. I never hear Zaydeh talk to my Bubbeh, never. And I've been coming to Bubbeh since kindergarten, so that makes fourteen years of Sundays, Zaydeh under-done days.

If I had magical powers, I could hold a glass up to the walls, eaves-drop on the squawking birds and find out what they think of Zaydeh or tell me why he keeps out of the kitchen.

Me, I sit at Bubbeh's kitchen table on a Sunday afternoon, watching her roll up the blistered blintzes, wrinkly cooked cabbage, or raw *kreplach plach* dough. With every move Bubbeh makes here, it's as if she's trying very hard to move closer to her husband and keep crazy Zaydeh pinned to her.

"Morris, take a bit of herring," she says. From his bedroom, the parlor, the bathroom, the basement, wherever he's hidden, Zaydeh hears her and runs, like a household pet, to the kitchen for his plate. He tousles my hair then gives me a little pat on the top of my head. Whenever he touches my head, my scalp itches the whole day. He asks, "You okay? You make okay in school?"

"Yes, Zaydeh. All As. But what I love most is cooking with Bubbeh."

He laughs. "You don't cook nothing. She does."

Zaydeh scares me. He is more than six feet tall and weighs almost 300 pounds, my Zaydeh, and has this huge, shiny bald head. His cold eyes, grayish and gleaming like his plumbing tools, make him look kind of mean. If Zaydeh were to play Animal, Vegetable or Mineral with us, he'd say he was a boulder. We walk around him, sidestep his long shadow. Not even the whole family together could push him hard enough to move him even the tiniest bit.

A minute later, Bubbeh pours Zaydeh's schnapps; with a simple head shake, he takes the glass, along with his plate, and just like that, he's gone.

"Bubbeh, does Zaydeh talk to you?"

"Talk? Sure. Vie not?"

"Well, what does he say?'

"Vutt should he say?"

"Words, Bubbeh, words."

"Vell, I get plenty words from him. 'Tank you,' 'Please,' 'Okay.' 'Enough' and 'I go.'"

Short, stingy words are what Bubbeh gets. Along with a big plateful of silence. Not the meaty, juicy words she deserves.

"Is that all, Bubbeh? Just a squawk, squawk here and a squawk, squawk there?"

"He makes a living. Does he have to make big talk, too?'

I try to ask what I'm asking another way. Like this: "When you met Zaydeh, what did you like best about him?"

She points to the floor. "Come, help. Bring to me da dustpan."

The broom and the dustpan, me and Bub. Swish, sweep, swoop, move back, move forward, sweep, swoop swoosh. We make it a game. Bubbeh and Zaydeh, well, I don't know what they make.

Ever since I was little, Jewish holidays meant a trip to Bubbeh's, who loves us at her house. Daddy says she's a very good housewife, but, me, I think she's indoors too much. So, a few years ago, when I was in fifth grade, the day after *Yom Kippor*, I pried Bub out of her kitchen and walked with her to the library. "Talk like the TV guy on "Dragnet," Bubbeh. Please. Jack Webb, your favorite actor." I skip alongside her.

"Ah-lo. Mine name is Sergeant Friday. And I'm a cup," she says.

This cracks me up every time. Mom gets a kick out of it, too, so we don't correct Bubbeh. Let Sergeant Friday be a "cup"; there are too many cops already. Once we reach the library, Bubbeh stops short at the wild Indian on his giant horse, a bronze statue outside the library. She lowers her head, and starts to pray aloud to the Indian. The wild Hebrew sounds she makes could just as well be Indian talk.

"What are you praying for, Bubbeh," I ask.

"For the books. I pray they will stay safe. Safe from fire, safe from hate."

"It's okay, Bubbeh. Let's go inside. No one burns books in our country," I stoop down, lift up the flap of a pretend box, and shout, "Nope, no Nazis here!" I get up quick so no one'll think I'm a fool. "Anyway, I only have ten vocab words to look up, so we'll be back before Zaydeh finishes up his plumbing job." She nods her head and smiles. Zaydeh likes his supper waiting for him on the stove. I hold the library door open for Bubbeh to follow me to the back.

That's where all the dictionaries and encyclopedias are.

The library smells like my clammy cellar when the clothes dryer hasn't been used for a while, smelling dank, but I don't mind, not with the big old windows that cover the long back wall of this rectangle. Staring straight back at the windows, I squint so I can see the dust dots better. Bubbeh and I both love light (my very first word as a baby). I do the setup: "Look, light, light!" What she's supposed to say back to me, in Yiddish, "Agezundah deine zight," means "God bless your eyesight."

Instead she asks. "V-here is Shakespeare?"

"He's way down, with the other "S" writers. This is where the regular books start. But we don't want them. We want non-fiction. Not made up stuff."

"You are bedda off mit Shakespeare, meine kinde."

How would she know that? "I need an in-sike-low-peed-e-a," I shout, as if Bubbeh's now hard of hearing "Truth, not stories."

"You can take da trutte from Shakespeare. A very vise man. My papa read him to me when I was young girl like you, read to me in Yiddish. I like best his poems. How you say in English?"

"He wrote plays, Bubbeh. Plays." I point to the hanging sign just ahead of us. "Reference. See? Atlases. Britannicas. Dictionaries. Facts, not stories. I need Truth Books, not the made up ones. Now do you see?"

"I see plenty trutte in Shakespeare." She points to the reference sign. "Dus is da friction. From Shakespeare, you get no fairy tales."

Her nose has begun to redden at the tip. Darn, I've said the wrong thing.

"Friction? Oh wait til I tell Daddy you said friction for fiction. He will howl! Listen, I'll do my stupid words, my definitions, and then Bubbeh, I'll get Shakespeare for you with my library card." There I go again, saying something kinda mean.

"I must make for Pa his supper," she says. Bub walks like a penguin, back and forth, back and forth.

Little me, I'm nearly out of breath trying to keep up with little Bubbeh on the ten short blocks from the library to her and Zaydeh's tenement house. Funny thing, I feel like I'm jumping out of my skin, jumping, jumping, jumping back and forth like crazy between fact and friction.

Next day, after school, I am setting Mom's hair in fat, wire rollers. "C'mon, Ma. Say something neat about when you were little. You had to like something else besides baseball."

Mom doesn't say much about growing up in the tenement house. You expect people to tell you childhood stuff, like what games they played, or what secrets they kept, or who they hung around with.

Except for stories about her dog, Skippy, Mom acts like she was born a grown-up. She liked what most girls did not: baseball, baseball, and baseball.

"Well, I loved to wake up to Bubbeh's special alarm, the sound of her calling my name." Turns out, Bub still makes the wondrous, hardy guttural "chaahk" (like the CH in BaCH) that kick-started my own mom's days.

"Chaya, Chaya," Bubbeh calls out twice, every time, for her middle daughter, whose English name, Irene, was not nearly as magical as her Yiddish one. For Chai means life and spirit and wild animal. And Mom is all of them, she is.

I love how the letter Chai goes trampling over Bubbeh's tonsils, mowing them back toward the bottom of her throat. Next thing I know, Chai soars from her kitchen, leaps out the window, and hop scotches down the driveway. Chai's Plain Jane counterpart, Irene, sticks to the back of your front teeth, parks there for the night, and conks you to sleep in sweaty day clothes, making my mother instead an ordinary girl trapped forever in a torch song, "Goodnight, Irene, I'll see you in my dreams."

"What else, Ma? What else did you do with Bubbeh and Zaydeh?" "Read. I loved to listen to her read aloud, I watch her point from left to right as she traced each word, forced the world to back track, reconsider its intent. But don't get me going now on her endearing ways."

Zip about Zaydeh.

"Me, I only get scared you won't always remember. So I figure I'll write stuff down for you, and they'll be there when you need them."

"Don't count me out so quickly, kiddo. I'm a tough old bird. How 'bout you make your own list?" She laughs, lights up a cig, does a quick exhale, and kisses me on the nose. "Go, your turn, again."

"This is too easy," I say. "Who combs down each side of my forehead with her fingertips, gives a quick lick to her pointer fingers, and then parts my imaginary hair? Bubbeh!" She is not very happy with her own hair, fine and curly; some sticks right to her head, the rest springs out. "Hair setting. Yup. That's something special with Bubbeh."

I think of my Bub handing me a comb and a sticky bottle of aqua hair gunk. She is looking into the bathroom mirror as she cluck, cluck, clucks. "'Make for me, please, my hair,' she'll always say, handing me the skinny comb. I stick it in the goop. "I can section her hair off really well, Mom, and twirl the little pieces around my finger into the skinniest, tightest pin curl." The silver pin curl holders shine like diamonds against her warm, marshmallow scalp. I can barely fit my little pinkie between the pin curls. If I could, I'd kiss my pinkie first, then press it into the tiny space.

"Your Bubbeh is so easy to do for. Isn't she?" Mom asks.

"Yes! Where Daddy is all tunnels and traps, *my* Bubbeh is all green lights," I say. Who else would let a young lady imitate her by filling the back pockets of my cheeks with sugar lumps, and then dissolving them with swishes of hot black coffee? My Bub-a-lah. And who still stuffs a teen's mouth with a hunk of *challah* so she won't sew up my soul as she's pinning up a piece of fallen hem or stitching a loose button on my cardigan?

I giggle. "Ma, I never saw a faster button put-er-on-er. Bubbeh can't wait for you to even change your clothes! She sews you on the spot."

"My momma is very, very careful with sharp needles and straight pins; she never stuck me once. You?" asks Mom.

"Never stuck me either! Good thing. I am a little petrified of pins." So petrified that even though I had a little crush on a Boy Scout, I quit Brownies as soon as I found out I had to earn stupid pins, and pin them all over your kerchief. Why push short, fat pins that might stub you?

Mom keeps her fancy dress pins at the bottom of her jewelry box. There sits a seal with diamond eyes, a squiggle pin of fake gold, a circle pin covered with pearls, a poodle pin with tiny pink stones on its ears, a shiny, silver baby-size Scottish Terrier, and a cute beagle dog pin with pretty fur made of baked enamel.

Much as she loves dogs, what with her best childhood friend a dog named Skippy, and Queenie, the mutt Daddy gave her on their fifth anniversary, she stuck herself on these ratty pins too many times to ever let these pretend dogs out.

I think whoever named safety pins is a fool; there's nothing safe about a pin. Except a pin that isn't a pin, like a rolling pin. This reminds me of baking, like the one Bubbelah uses to make us goodies. Her kitchen is a beauty parlor where everything gets gussied up. I wish everyone could see her braid challah! Two Fridays ago, I watched as she tucked in the braid's tails, and then washed its face with an egg yolk to make it shine. Okay, challah does not have a real face, but so what? But here's the best part. I ask her to spell the word "challah" for me every time she makes it, a trick I have to get her to say my second favorite Bub sound: chet.

Challah's first letter choo-choos its way to Shabbat. Lucky me, I got to sleep over Bub and Zaydeh's that Friday. I lay on the couch for a while with my head propped up, just so I could hear him say something to her in their married bed. Nuttin.

So, I played my War of the Word game until I felt very sleepy. I started with Chet. To make my own Chet sound as good as Bubbeh's, I pretend the tip of my throat is in a big battle with the bottom of it. I even have Chet fencing with his enemy! The sword swooshes 'chet, chet, chet.' In other words, take that and that and that, you crazy, *goyisha* swashbuckler, you!" I know this is a lot of work for one letter to do, but Chet's a good sport.

I look over at Mom, her head stuck in the sports page again.

She reads aloud: "'Good news for Boston fans today. Boston and Detroit are tied for first.' She smiles over at me. "Get this. When Ted Williams burst out of the dugout, the crazy bastard flipped the bird at the fans three times. Once to the left, once to the middle, once to the right. That's his trademark. Natch, he stepped out of the box to spit at fans on his next up.'

"The Splendid Splitter is at it again," I say, jump up from the divan and fence with a pretend enemy in the air. Then it's off to school.

Horrible, horrible news today. Carrying a load of whites down cellar," as my mama would say, my *Bubbelah* tripped and broke her cooking arm. All this just three days after my last sleep over there. No cooking with Bubbeh this week. Who knows how long? She must stay in the hospital; only grown-ups can visit.

"Who is cooking for Zaydeh?"

"The devil. Not a bad cook either," says Mom. "If we're lucky, his favorite spice is arsenic."

I laugh. Silently I say, Zaydeh, Zaydeh, why'd you make Mom hate 'ya?

"Tell you what," says Mom, cradling my head. "I will give Bubbeh a special kiss every day from you. Tell me where to kiss, I will kiss."

Kissing my own head now, she doles out pecks all over. "Here, no here, yeah there, there, that's Bubbeh's favorite kissing zone."

She retreats, fishes for the goods in the pocket of her apron, and announces "Two ciggies left to last all night." She means: one now; one for the middle of the night. Most every night, I hear her in the middle of the night getting up to smoke, coughing on the first drag, and crying on the last.

The next morning, I'm brushing my teeth when I hear Mom downstairs singing and washing the breakfast dishes. What she always sings is snippets from her favorite Sophie Tucker song. Like these:

"My Yiddishe Momme, I need her more than ever now. My Yiddishe Momme, I long to kiss her wrinkled brow. I long to hold her hand once more as in days gone by. And ask her to forgive me for the things I did to make her cry."

Only Mom's not the one who makes her Yiddishe Momme cry. If it's anyone, it's him, the murderer, him, the dog killer. It's him, "House Devil, Street Angel." It's him, Morris Goldstein, Plumber." It's him, smelly cigar smoker, who chased his son, my Uncle Mucko, round and round the apartment, threatening to cut his fingers off one at a time—with his stupid cigar cutter—if he ever dated a goy again. "Jeepers," I say to Daddy, "When am I going to see Bub? She's been in the hospital forever." Daddy and I are bringing Mom's groceries in from the garage. Daddy puts his two bags down, just like that, on the cement floor. I look down, and see Daddy's bare feet on the cold concrete. He has on Bermuda shorts, and a collared shirt. This is the dress of a medium-down Daddy. Either on his way back up to being Up Daddy or halfway back down to being a fully Down Daddy.

But for this month, let's call Medium-Rare Daddy, a decent Daddy who does chores around the house, like carry in the grocery bags, take up the laundry, bring in the newspaper, take out the garbage. He talks small, too. Looking at Mom, he asks, "Irene? Right time? Wrong time? No matter." I don't get the code.

"You're right, Joey. C'mon, keep me company, Marlenala, and help me put this stuff away. I have some news."

"Yippee. Bubbeh's ready? Ready for home? Is that what Daddy means?"

"You know how I always kiss her on the head for you?" She's staring at Daddy, not me. "Bandage-bandage is what I kiss. Feh! That's what keeps Bub's head warm. Bandage. Two surgeries already, trying to stop the bleeding. Her head was banged up kind of bad."

I scream, "Not her head, no!" Not that pretty pinkness beneath the curls. No. Bandage means glue. Glue means stuck. No. Stuck to hair, glue, that will rip out when the bandage comes off. "Poor, poor Bubbeh! Is her brain—well, is it all right?"

Mom sighs loudly. "Yes, she will be fine. She will."

"Stop talking to me like I'm a baby. I am not a baby. I never was. You said so yourself. That I was born old. Just like you. It's what you said."

"God forgive me, I hate that son of a bitch. Hate 'im!"

It's then I notice that Mom's lit another cigarette when one's already in the ashtray. Her body shakes as if she's ice cold. Crying now like me, she lifts a corner of her apron to her nose and blows hard. I wrap my arms around her. "Ma, don't cry. Please. Don't cry."

For some crazy reason, what I say makes Mom smirk. "Listen, wise guy, you're already playing wet nurse to one parent. Two you don't need." Next thing I know, she is sliding out our "Mental Drawer." You know, the one crazy space in every kitchen where you shove everything. She fishes for something, comes up with a raggedy looking newspaper. Pointing toward the dining room, she asks me to come sit with her at the table.

She opens up and flattens the *Worcester Daily Telegram*. Mom has folded and unfolded this newspaper so many times that it's ripped in two places. It reminds me of the Fortune Tellers us kids make by creasing and folding and folding a large sheet of paper into one small square. You flip up a triangle and reveal your entire future (Love, Hate, Friendship, Kiss, Court or Marriage). I thought, so here comes Bubbeh's future.

"Made the front page." Mom points to six small words in big letters:

"CITY COUPLE FOUND HURT IN HOME"

"Burglars?"

She shakes her head no. Starts to read: "An elderly couple was hospitalized this morning, one in critical condition." I pray the "one" is Zaydeh, Mr. Morris Goldstein. Awful of me, I know.

"Mrs. Bessie Goldstein, 66, was taken to City Hospital in the police ambulance blah, blah, blah the victim of a brutal beating. She was suffering from severe cuts to the head, face and scalp."

She pounds the paper down, slaps it hard twice, as if she could bury it right in the coffee table.

"And Zaydeh? Did they get him, too?"

"Got, not get." Mom says, "They've got the bastard behind bars." She takes a long drag off her cigarette, then stubs it out. "Something's burning."

"Ma! You missed the ashtray." The table is what's burning. With her bare fingernail, she scratches at the black gunk in the new burn hole, then covers it up with her ashtray.

This is no future I've ever seen on a paper Fortune Teller, that's for sure. "Please, Mom, just read."

"'A half hour later, a second ambulance was called to the Dorchester Street address. Mrs. Goldstein's husband, Morris, also 66, was found injured in the cellar of the house. He had a cut on the head and a gash on the left wrist, which authorities termed superficial.'"

What I'm thinking is how different Zaydeh's blood, dark and oily like calf's liver, must be from Bub's blood, so bright, light and, just like a juicy cherry pop.

"They did get him, too! Yes? And the rats are behind bars, right?" "So and so is investigating, and so and so called the police. It was Isaac Klein, who said he heard groans frthfirst floor apartment of the Goldsteins. Klein found Mrs.

Goldstein on the floor of her bedroom, police said. Mrs. Gillus, the upstairs tenant, called headquarters again after discovering Mr. Goldstein in the cellar. Police reported finding a blood-smeared hammer nearby."

"Enough with the blood already. Enough." Mom holds the newspaper over her heart.

What I'm thinking now is that the robbers hit Bubbeh first, and Zaydeh, no dummy, went right to his plumbing tools, grabbed the hammer, and smashed the bad guy's head in. The other bad guy wrestled the hammer from Zaydeh, punched his lights out, threw him down the stairs, and for spite, tried to pin it on Zaydeh. That's it! That's why the hammer was down cellar with Zaydeh.

I take the paper from my Mother and skim right through to the end and read: "Morris Goldstein has been charged with a deadly assault by sledgehammer." I need to know exactly what this is, so I leap up to the dictionary stand. Here's what I read aloud to Ma: "Adjective. Sledgehammer: Ruthlessly severe; crushing." (If I had to look up the word "he," I bet I would find only this: noun, Zaydeh.)

"Crushing, *meine kinde*? You don't know the half of it. Crushed my Mama's skull into a million pieces! Held together with pins now. Pins, for Chrissakes."

I only see pin curls: I cannot picture pin pins.

"Jewish men do not beat on their wives, Mom, right? They make the best husbands, right? You said so."

"Your Bubbeh is still in critical condition, honey, but the doctors say she's a fighter, that she could come out of this just fine. Imagine. Fifteen hours of surgery." "Brain surgery? Or just surgery on the outside, ya know—outside of her head." I can't stop crying, can't stop thinking of this plush pink head that I kissed and kissed and kissed and still could not love it enough, this wonderful head that became a crazy man's coconut, that sweet pink meat all banged and bloodied up, pressed back together, and shoved back inside by strangers, by doctors, who did not know the woman crying inside.

But all I could say to Mom was, "How long before Bubbeh's hair grows back? How long before I can make her pin curls?"

"Don't know, honey. Just don't. Come, by the television. It'll help us escape. The Red Sox play at home tonight. Last game he was ejected, my Jimmy."

I turn the knob on, and there he is, our *meshugenah* neighbor, sucking up all the space on the screen. One booming boo is what I hear from those faraway muffles of voices, like the voices you hear when you close your eyes at the beach. "What's he done now, Mom?"

"Nothing yet. Jimmy's still taking the heat from Sunday's double-header. Mickey Mantle was up at bat. The goddamn Yank that he is, he made a big stink over Piersall's little scurry back and forth across the outfield. Umps threw Jimmy out for trying to quote distract the batter. End quote."

"Boo, boo, boo, boo," I squeal at the heel on the screen.

"Shush! What the matter with you, Marlene-ala? Thirty thousand fans show up to boo Piersall. They need you, too?"

I have never seen from our noisy neighbor what I am seeing now: a Jimmy who stands perfectly still. As if his Daddy had said, "Don't move a muscle." Finally. He is pinned to his post in centerfield. Yup, pinned. Years later, Jimmy would go on to play the shallowest centerfield in the majors; he would win two Golden Gloves. A two-time All Star, Jimmy would be labeled one of the best defensive outfielders of his era. One day Casey Stengel himself would call J.P. a better

Defensive outfielder than Joe DiMaggio. In his 17 seasons, with nearly 4,000 chances, peripatetic Piersall would make fewer than forty errors.

But the day the truth came out about my Bubbeh's pins, well, that day I was glad for the five minutes I saw Piersall pinned, too. As if Jimmy, head bowed, had shown us how sorry he was for my family. As if he had slowed down long enough to love us back, as if he knew we were nearly fresh out of it for our own Daddies.

# 12

# Suiting Up

Jimmy Piersall's darkened home, all shadowy and sinister, seems to come at you through the glow of a gaslight. Me, I think Piersall may be playing tricks, gaslighting his home, and dimming the lights at crazy times. All to drive his wife mad, just like that movie husband did. Or maybe to torture the babysitter?

Mom pooh-poohs me. I throw an afghan over myself teepee style and start toward our door.

"I hate to ruin your latest story, Miss Sentence Maker, but Jimmy probably just forgot about the bill," Mom says, "missed the shut-off notice. Take a flashlight."

Tonight, for sure, I'm asking flat out why it's nearly pitch black there. Heck, I'll say they owe me the reason, right along with my 35 cents an hour.

I can't abide the lack of light. Waited all week to use that word, abide. The bellies of the "b" and the "d" pair off, ready for tango; the dance in my mind makes me a little woozy. Still, I'll try out abide on Mrs. Piersall.

Walking across our driveway to theirs, I claw and jab my way through the dark, short stretch of the Piersall's lawn, counting out loud. Thirteen steps to the front step. I press forward and knock, knock at the front door. That's when I stub my toe and nearly fall into their foyer.

"Hi Ho, Missy Marlene," says Mrs. Piersall. "I left the door open for you. Figured the TV might light your way."

"Ouch," I say, hopscotching and grabbing for my foot.

"Bright lights give my husband even more horrible headaches. You won't ever see the Piersalls' lawn strewn with Christmas lights, that's for sure. Let alone a light bulb in the lamppost. Gosh. Where did November go all ready?"

"No Christmas tree? Not even without lights?" This, to a Jewish teenage girl, an outsider who only wants one once a year, now shortchanged! This, this I will not abide. Just for the shortest minute I want to strangle Mrs. Piersall with her fat white strand of pearls. White, of course.

"Your foot okay?" she says. "No, no Christmas here. Oh we'll put our tree up in February when Jimmy's down at spring training. My husband's already in the garage, dear, waiting for me. I'll just grab my purse and say goodnight to the girls."

My eyes stay on her as she swoops down to kiss the girls. When she gets up, I recognize the small square she holds in front of her, just like a bouquet, is her purse.

I can't tell Deenie and Eenie apart in this ink well, even with the TV on. Eight skinny limbs on trees, like branches against snow, that's who they are. One girl flips channels: 5, 7 and 12; 12, 10, 5; I catch Eenie's face in the flickers. Glad or sad, you wouldn't know.

When you can't see, you can smell. Underneath, a burnt, oily, sickish sweet. A wallpaper paste smell on top. Or is it baking soda, cornstarch, flour and water? Wait. It is. It is Swanson's Fried Chicken dinner all right, gluey mashed potatoes and limp corn again at the Piersall corral.

"Finish up, girls," I say to the back of their heads. "I don't want to step on boney chicken bones again. I already stubbed my toe."

Deenie's voice: "Got a flash light if you need to go pee-pee. We don't need light bulbs. Halloween at our house lasts longer than Christmas. That's what our Daddy says."

Eenie's voice: "You should see our Daddy unscrew the light bulbs, wrap them up in a towel, and stomp on 'em, stomp, stomp, stomp. Jewish people do that for good luck."

Deenie's voice: Don't you like it better when our Daddy baseball bats 'em bulbs to death!"

Eenie's voice: You would! I like the Jewish person stomping a whole lot better.

I say nothing.

It's then I figure if I want a big tip, I better be nicer. Ask the girls what's on their Chistmas lists, so I settle down to the floor, nestle up to the girls and ask what they want for Christmas. Tea sets, make-up heads, trucks, baseball gear. Next time, I'll ask them about their favorite movie stars, and the time after that, what kind of candy.

"Girls, wash up. Brush your teeth." And they pop up like toast! One behind the other, holding onto her sister's waist, choo-chooing it, blind man's bluffing it, to their bunk beds.

Mrs. Piersall has asked me to sit again for her after school the next day. That'll also be the first night of Chanukkah, so I get to keep busy by babysitting in the daylight, dreaming about my presents to come. Jimmy's still shut up inside that house somewhere. In his bedroom, I figure.

"Dear, I am just going to the market and then the post office. Please, please keep the girls as quiet as you can."

I ask, "Is Mr. Piersall regular sick, or is he, um, troubled."

"Not exactly troubled. More like restless. He can't sit still; he can't lay down. He's got pounding headaches. Can't get any relief."

But why didn't Piersall rest in November? It's what Mom screams when the Sox get sloppy. "C'mon, you lousy bums," Mom says. "What is it you're waiting for, huh? Bear down on this Moose, for crying out loud. You got plenty of time to rest in November."

Moose Skowron swings for the Yankees. He's a tough one to put away. Jimmy likes to stick his tongue out at him, waving his fingers behind his ears. This reminds me to ask Mom what's so special about November.

She lights up, exhales, and grins. "It's a saying, mommelah. Oh, it's like saying,'C'mon, c'mon. Up off your tuchuses!' Wait until November for your rest!"

That afternoon, Mary Piersall greets me with a hug. She starts like this: "Jim was practically born with a sickness. When he starts pounding at his temples, it means his head's about to explode. He's talking to himself in the dark all night long. Trying to talk down the headache, talk himself to sleep."

Headaches like that? I'd be thinking brain tumor. In a Jewish body, all roads lead to cancer. Sore elbow? Elbow cancer. To be precise: Bone cancer of the elbow.

"Oh! All ball players are restless in November. Can't wait until spring training. I have a surprise for you."

Emphatically I say, "Rest in November. He's not supposed to be restless. Headaches could be serious." Brain tumor, brain tumor brain tumor. No wonder Jimmy's in such bad humor. (Bad pun, granted).

"I've already wrapped your Chanukkah present! Here. Go ahead. Oh, I do hope you'll like it."

A blouse. No, a very white blouse. My Mom used to say making anything white, like white clothes, white houses, and especially white sox, is a waste of a color."Very *goyish*, white is, she has told me more than once. Even ten years later, I will say, "Me? I cannot abide white."

"Thank you, Mrs. Piersall. This is so-so white. I love it. I specially love white uniforms." I reel them off: "Mrs. Ellis the school nurse, Mr. Clean. The whirling white T-shirted cleaning giant trapped in a bottle, Morris Daniels the dentist, Meyer the baker, Casper the Friendly Ghost. Mitzy the butcher. Lone Ranger and his white stallion. Good Humor Man." Soon as I've made my list, I figure I may as well have shortened it to "I hate white uniforms."

"I love the look of a uniform, don't you?' sings Mrs. Piersall.

U N I F O R M . Pulling the word out, then reigning it in, the accordion sound of Mrs. Piersall's "uniform" makes it a much different word than mine.

"Uniforms, yes, they are magic" she says. She closes her eyes. Maybe she sees Jimmy backing up to the Green Monster, trolling centerfield forever, for a team almost impossible to put away. She imagines the saltiness of his hips as he shimmies into position. She bends her mind between his legs, spread wide apart, and finds she has just now put her own left foot forward. Imaginary glove on left knee, right hand on right knee, while all the while, inside her Jimmy she is.

No one, I thought back then, could ever hit one over the head of this center fielder in front of me. You find nothing shallow in Mary Piersall's plays.

Daylight magnifies the best stuff in our kitchen; even the linoleum looks hopeful, as if it were waiting for a walk-on woman with a broom to sweep it up into a commercial. In the bright morning sun, even the crumbs on the counters swell like precious ore; all rough edges shine like they'd been dipped in mica. Our beagle's scattered brown, blonde and white dog hairs turn into copper, gold and silver, finally giving our beloved mutt, Queenie, the royal status her name had promised. Mom is at the sink, scrubbing the tuna casserole; the soap suds are prisms. The flood of light softens and whitens that wonderful squishy, floppy skin under Mom's arms, turning them into swinging marshmallow pillows. In a sad house like ours, you'd think we'd look worse lit up like this.

Especially Daddy. But no. Facing me, seated on the bench at the breakfast nook, Daddy grins at me, then winks. The light has fattened up his little smile and widened his wink. He raises his head, points to his cheek. I kiss his cheek, now a pillow in a satin pink pillow case, and silently recite my Bubbeh's first blessing of my first baby girl word:

"Y- I -G- H - T! Y- I - G- H - T!"

To which Daddy shouts, "God bless your eyesight." (Daddy has read my mind; in the flood of light around me, everything is transparent and clear).

I grab the opportunity: "Daddy, move over. Bet you could use a little help on your crossword, huh?"

Only now am I sorry about the light. It shows that Daddy, like Jimmy, is still resting. He wears his flimsy, formless uniform: the back of his boxer shorts go in front, and stupid see-through, ribbed old-man T shirts. Why they call them muscle shirts, when they line his little pot like celery strings, I'll never know. I don't know either who gets to make up the good man-man names like trousers, but Daddy's legs, crossed and shaking like the trolley, are not easy to contain.

When I get home from school, Daddy has wriggled his way into a pair of rumpled trousers, *shlumpy* frayed collar shirt, and wraps up tightly in a pilled gray cardigan from my Aunt Norma, three sizes too large, her newest old gift. After dinner, he's T-shirted and boxered in for the night.

Daddy took his first lay-down, long-time rest when I was in third grade. Now I count back: three rests in March, three rests in April, three rests in May. Once, a rest all summer long. But November? This is a first. By my count, he's been in bed since Mom's Veteran's Day birthday. Right now all I want to do is hibernate with Daddy.

High-burr-nate. It's middle syllable sounds exactly like what it stands for (I love it when a word does smart things like that with itself). What are the odds I can convince Down Daddy to hibernate, say, half a year with me? Strictly an experiment. Would we waken in spring as good as new? Would the long rest melt his melancholy like fat for fuel?

Hibernating Daddy and Daughter will change into two tiny groundhogs, swirl and swirl about and finally, settle in together. We won't need to breathe even, let alone pee or poop. Hibernators don't digest.

I read where, if you're really old and sick and bedridden, your bones get all brittle-ey. Not so for hibernating bears: they lift their big fat *tuchuses up, and walk crisp and brisk, like they've never been off their* feet. Come May, we'll dig out and hop home. Just by putting us to sleep for one lousy winter, I could get Daddy a new life.

I wake him up at 11:30 am on Sunday. "Hey, I say, I think I could take what I know about hibernation and apply it to people one day. Say, put them into hibernation until cures for their various diseases are found. Shut them down sick, warm them up well."

If he minds my waking him with whacky ideas like this, who knows? He smiles or fake-laughs. Doesn't say but a word or two. But I'm happy with the few words he has stored up. I shoot a two-pager conversation at him, and Daddy has to answer me with three, four sentences, a puny paragraph. Me: Blah, blah, blah, you wouldn't believe Bruce Berman, trying to wrestle his ruler under my under thingy and Blah blah ate the soggy smelly turkey pot pie, but left the crust alone. Blah filled up another composition book.

All I ever really want to hear is what he says when he first sees me.

Even with his smile lines pulled back by the invisible puppeteer, his face muscles soften, his eye bags dangle carefree, and his wincing twin almonds of sadness—his eyes—round just the littlest bit. What he has to say, and say it he does every time I walk through the door, all he really has to say is: "Hi there, little yellow bird. Hope you had a good day at school. Did you learn a lot?"

The fake fairy tales I tell him in return always give him an out.

"Another A in French! I myself just got home. Turned up quite a job. A definite maybe. All the coffee drinking at the interview gave me heartburn, hon, so I'll say my good night early. Don't forget to say your *Shema* before you go to sleep."

3:30 pm. He won't get up again until morning, when Mom will beg, "Come, Joey, have a nice warm cup of coffee. Just finished brewing this minute."

But Daddy shouts back that his esophagus is out of whack. Hot coffee would set it on fire.

Right before my favorite holiday, just as magically as drowsiness set in, nowhere really I could name, pep steps in and takes its place. Just like that: rest over, done, finis. Here it is almost Chanukkah, festival of lights, and boom! Daddy's all color and heat, like the candles. I hold his chin close and Eskimo kiss his long, waxy, warm nose dressed in his navy blue, Bar Mitzvah and wedding suit, a sharp looking drip-dry poplin, plus his white collared shirt with a navy bow tie, Daddy stands in the kitchen, sipping coffee, and holding a newly creased *Boston Globe*.

He beams when he sees me. "Wow!"

He bows. "No regular flannel suits for Top Dollar Joe, no sir-ee." With his right hand, he grabs and clutches at the air. Or is the Pup-peteer responsible for that?

Still, calling himself by his old success of a name, well, this sounds pretty good to me. As if Daddy might finally be swallowing up the fake Daddies who'd already taken their turns tormenting him. I'm hoping he'll even swallow up Joey

Rosenfield, along with Joey Fields—his alias when writing or calling city officials—and his imposter gangster self, but no, not today.

"But show me a high-button flannel, a Nehru collar, then you can deal me in, Yellow Bird," says the gambling gangster.

Presto, the invisible Puppeteer lifts up Daddy's head, and gets working his face muscles. Yuk. Now Daddy even looks like a gambling man: his eyes half shut and his lips screwed to one side as if to say, "I don't smile 'regular'. See? See? Nothing regular about your Daddy, nothing at all."

"Listen to this one, my little yellow bird."

Why else would he call me a bird, his own yellow bird, were he not still a looney bird?

I'm on the wing, he has said to me dozens of times. And to me, that meant, me, not him. I was on his wing, or he was always right by my side. On my side. I'd be a year older before I realized that's not what he meant. Not at all. He meant he was ready for take-off, ready to fly. Down Daddy, fly, fly, bye, bye.

And this yellow bird, even though now a sixteen-year old, well, she, she would have clipped your wings, Up Daddy, first time you gave her any lip. For she knew, as far back as her infancy, she knew what giving any lip at all could do. Too much lip, too seldom silence. Come then all the violence.

But as for the jibber jabber Daddy I had back then? Listen to him, will ya:

"Honey, dig this Help Wanted! "Quote: 'Sales Manager. Intangible experience must be able to move efficiently at top management level and effectively understand—capital B's—Big Businesses' problems. Should be able to handle martini luncheons with grace and dignity.'"

"They pay you to drink, Daddy?" I hate them.

"You got it wrong, honey. It's all about loosening up. They want a fellow to be loose, see? To take a guy from out of town out for dinner, and not be a wet blanket. They don't want a *schmendrick* in a gray flannel suit. They want cordovans, lace-ups, not penny loafers or slip-ons. That's for saps. Now here's the tricky part. They're looking for a clean-cut company man on the outside, and a killer in the inside."

"Daddy, you look so handsome. You look like Top Dollar Joe!"

Again, Daddy summoned up his favorite nickname for himself, one he chose as the name for the huge car lot he owned once, back when he had not just money but a heap of hope.

"Top Dollar Joe, am I right? Your ole man is a go-getter on the go. Wait 'til I show them the stuff I'm made of. Don't you see? I move ideas. It's what I do. Give your Daddy a peck for good luck," he said, puffing out his check and tapping it twice with his tattooed, letter "O" ring finger. The "O" and "D" on the fingers to the right; the letter "G," natch, is on the pinkie. G-O-O-D.

He never taps with his "L-U-C-K" hand.

Just before dinner, I find Daddy at the kitchen table, taking notes from a really fat book. "See this? *The Insurance Man's Guide to Success*. I got homework, too, sweetheart. You know why? Because Joe got himself a job today. I am an American. I live in a country where any man can be a success. Yellow bird, you're looking at the next member of the Million Dollar Round Table." He sighs, shuts the book, clicks his Paper Mate, and pushes his chair out from the table.

Standing up, Daddy puts his hands in his pockets. "Ah, you never dream you'd end up a certain way and then, one day, a certain way seems like the only way."

I didn't have to look to know his next move. Clasping his hands together behind him and rocking himself on the tip toes of his cordovans. I don't think Daddy likes his hands much. He may even be ashamed of them. Quick as he can, he gets them out of the way. He stuffs one in a pocket; cups the other across his belly. He sits on them when he watches TV. He drinks with a straw and keep his hands off the glass. That's not easy to do. He shoves them in gloves when it's not even cold out. The only thing I can't figure out is why he sets his arms out real straight and cracks his knuckles, putting his hands right out there where everyone can see them. Right after a good click, click, karack, he winces, and stuffs the bullying tattooed fingers right back in his pockets.

I make a grab for my library book, *Death of a Salesman*. I begin at the end, as if I'm reading Torah. Only by reading the book backwards could you turn Willy Loman's luck around.

"Daddy, I love Willy Loman. I love when Charley explains a true salesman. 'He's a man out there in the blue, riding on a smile and a shoeshine.' I stop before the next line, the one about earthquakes, about being all washed up.

"A salesman is got to dream, boy." I shout, and slam the book shut in triumph. In my version, all this stuff comes at the beginning of *Death of a Salesman*. Not at the end.

"I'm no Willy Loman. He drank his poison and left his family holding the bag. No, Joe Rosenfield is made of very different stuff." Daddy makes a face I've seen him make with relatives, but never with me. It's the one where he separates his smile in two; one half grins; the other, the left half, tugs down as if his mouth is attached again to that darn puppet string; he tilts his head to the right. Another puppet string move, compliments of the invisible Puppeteer.

"Salesman, shmales-man, no more Fails Man. That's me. Bet you I sell my first million bucks worth of life insurance, I'm in the Roundtable, dig?"

That's his Bohemian talk! I "dig" when I get that point. We "split" for the grocery store. Splitting is something I love to do with Daddy. There's usually a little present in it for me.

He already looks lost, frightened maybe. "I have dreamed another dream. Who said that?" Daddy asks.

"You?" I ask.

"Joseph. The crazy cat who wore a coat of many colors. No wonder I'm named after him. Sonuva bitch." He smirks.

"Torah Joseph?" This from a Daddy who tried to pass for Protestant twice, ate pork in public to further his disguise, and hung up quotes from the Preacher, Norman Vincent Peale: "Become a possibilitarian. No matter how dark things seem to be, raise your sights and see possibilities. They're right there in front of you."

Myself, I hate the Peale Squeal. It figures: Peale's always wearing a white starched shirt, with a do-nothing white triangle popping out of his suit pocket. But, it doesn't matter a lick what I do or say tonight. No one can keep this Joseph in his manger.

"Gotta split," he says. "Tell Mom not to wait up."

A few minutes later, I find Mom in the laundry room; she's turned the basket upside down and made it her seat. Mom's got *The Boston Globe* sports section in one hand, a butt in the other.

"Nice work, Mom," I tease, and point to the three skinny lines of ash in the tray on the floor in front of her feet.

"My work in progress. Remind you of anything, these stripes? Say, like the ones the traitorous Yankees sport on their uniforms? Oh, your Aunt Norma popped in this morning. You know, the woman who starred in the motion picture. "I Wake up Screaming"? Norma wore her usual colors: dark and darker. Let's see. I want to get this just right. Yes, quote, commission is for the goyim. End quote."

I say, "You told her Massachusetts Blue Chip is trying Daddy out in sales first? That he'll be sales manager before we know it?"

My mother snorts a little. "What I told her is, 'next time give a call before you come over.'"

We have proof: Daddy's fat, first commission check means he's sold a ton of insurance in his first two weeks. As a joke, he plunks the check down on my empty dessert plate. "Now serving fresh, hot moolah," he says.

Mom's plate has the envelope. "Gee, Joey, I was hoping for some hot apple pie and vanilla ice cream." Her grin is so wide that her cheeks look like parentheses.

"For you, my dear, an entire apple orchard, plus a milking cow for the cream. Queenie, after what I put you through, well." His nose twitches. "Joe that was yesterday's news. Today is a different story." She reaches across the table as if she wants to hold his hand. Instead, she takes his dessert spoon and raps on the table. Yeah, yeah. Knock on wood.

I wish she had his hand instead. Held it even for a minute. But I doubt Daddy likes anyone to hold his hand, what with that hand mishe-gas he's got going. And Mom? She does not touch Daddy in front of me. Maybe not even behind me.

Something's up. Even though Daddy only sleeps three, four hours a night, he wakes up all perky-shmerkey. Mom and I both pester him: she about talking less; me about sleeping more.

Our faces pucker like two little old *tantehs* (aunts).

"Stop worrying about me, both of youse. Please. You go back to doing whatever it is that terrible teenagers are supposed to do, and you, Irene, my baseball Queen, you start rooting for the real power hitter. Top Dollar Joe." He rises, plants a kiss on my curly top, and winks. "Next week, I'll start to draw salary on top of commission, Irene. Salary. Imagine that. One more week. And be eligible for free life insurance on myself. That's great, no? It's all about the power of positive thinking is what I'm thinking."

Worth more dead than alive, Willy Loman is. On account of on word: insurance.

Daddy faces the lower kitchen cabinet and frisks for his booze. With his free hand behind his back, he pulls open the fridge, and feels for a cold one. Guzzling down a boilermaker, he lassoes the phone with his right hook.

Boilermaker. Just what boils? Just what is do you make? Boiler-maker, heart-breaker, take-it-backer, that's what. Back in third grade, when he had Top Dollar Joe's cars, I remember his setting a little glass of whiskey next to a mugful of beer. He'd down the whiskey, then the beer. Maybe I was in second grade? I saw the fixings for fresh boilermaker on the red-and-pink Formica kitchen counter for months and months. Two different glasses, one short, one tall, both filled with honey liquid: one bubbling and airy; the other syrupy and somber. Together, a magical concoction. Deep breath, and down the hatch goes the gold. Potent one, long sigh, potent two.

But now, tonight, Daddy dumps a dollop of whiskey—straight from the bottle—into his beer stein. He does not explain why. I figure it's about efficiency. One potent worker faster than two separate ones. Ker-Blam.

Still, what is this poisonous boiling all about? And why does the boil go cold so quickly? Why can't Daddy just stay on a slow simmer and sell the stupid insurance.

No boilermaker in my *Webster's* or our *Britannica's*. Ah. It's in the *Better Homes and Garden's Party Book*. "When poured one into the other, the boilermaker creates a depth charge." My heart races, and I reread it slowly. Whew. First I thought it said death charge, which is an easy mistake to make, it being just one letter change and all. I find "depth charge" in my *Britannica*.

Only what I read scares me. "A charge designed for detonation at a pre-set depth under water, used especially against submarines. Also referred to as depth bomb."

Three boilermakers later, Daddy calls my uncles, his cousins, the kosher butcher, his dentist, Mom's hairdresser, and all my junior high school teachers.

Just before beddy-bye, I find Daddy's dog-eared *The Power of Positive Thinking, a Practical Guide to Mastering the Problems of Everyday Living.* Shuffling quickly through the Peale deck of dreck, I wonder if any one of the zillion listeners who tune into his weekly radio show ever even thought of hibernation. All that positive imaging could work up one heck of a headache. I say my prayers in bed, and pray that Daddy will have his business suit on way after New Year's.

Meanwhile, I suspect Jimmy has a different uniform (an ambulance took him away on Christmas). Still, I couldn't figure out why Piersall, who bellowed his way around the bases, suddenly shut right up. Mary Piersall visited him every day, but told us he hadn't spoken a word in five weeks. Did silence prove him crazier or saner?

Him? Him who?

Down Daddy and Away Jimmy, that's who.

He wears a uniform, all right. Only he's not suited up for the Sox.

Away Jimmy has been put away.

I did not see the ambulance and the men in the white coats (white, natch) come for Jimmy, but Mom stopped by the Piersalls every night, after supper, to check on Mary Piersall. She took her a plate sometimes, usually a hunk of Dirty Meatloaf, one of Mary's favorites. (Daddy calls it Doody Meatloaf on account of its texture and color) but what Mary likes the most are Mom's ciggies. Yup, two hours after the ambulance took Jimmy away, Mrs. Piersall mooched her first cig-arette from Ma. Blowing smoke rings and trying to outdo each other, mostly they giggled together.

I asked, "What's so funny?" what with her husband being a mental case.

"It's what you do, mommelah, when you can't speak about what's, well, unspeakable."

Back then, our family kept time in baseball seasons. Once Jim returned to baseball, and had a decent number of seasons behind him, Mom could spill the beans. I took down every word. From her stories about Jimmy hospitalization, and later, from Jimmy's own book about his breakdown, *Fear Strikes Out*, I would write about the season, winter 1952, we had lost him.

Like this:

Standing with his nose pressed against the bars of the Violent Room window at Westborough State Hospital, just forty minutes from our houses, Jimmy fixes on a gigantic silver water tower and repeats his Rosary. Next he prays to St. Joseph, patron saint of families, and then to St. Anthony, patron saint of lost things.

"St. Anthony, St, Anthony, please look around, something is lost, which cannot be found."

He repeats it twice.

"Please, help me find my glove. Have to find it. My glove. I can't practice without it, now can I? Can't very well find it myself in this god awful suit. My hands. My hands."

He imagines his fingers molding into the web of the glove. Hands now flattened by the crazy suit, the strait jacket they've used to bench him here, here in the Violent Room.

"Those sneaks flew me to Sarasota, they did, all this way, mind you, get me to Florida and then go and hide my glove on me. Then the Sox—sonsabitches— went and hid my uniform. Stole it from my hotel closet while I was getting a little shuteye.

Mind you, I stay shut up in that hotel room, with my roommate, they always give you a roommate, I stay maybe four or four days, waiting like a kid for his mommy to pick him up, waiting for Red Sox Boss Bou-dreau or, or maybe one of the coaches, waiting here for any darn fool to get on the horn and tell me to suit up. Report to Payne Field. Order me to go to shortstop.

And I will say to whichever crazy bastard says it, I'll say, 'I'm no shortstop, bud. A man needs his glove. No glove, no baseball. Maybe that's what they want. Red Sox do not want me to play any ball. So they shift me to shortstop, hide my glove, and make darn sure I can't. Soon as St. Anthony helps me, frees me from this strait jacket and helps me find my glove, fuck 'em all, I'll sign on with Topping and Web and preen in centerfield in my pinstripes."

A month later, in a private room, his hands free, Piersall wakes to a short, stubby man in a white (naturally) coat who asks, "Do you know where you are right now, Mr. Piersall? Do you know that you've been sick?"

"How long have I been out of my head, Doc?"

"You've been with us since early January. Going on six weeks now." "No headache. A miracle. Praise the Lord." He propels himself forward and touches his toes. Gone. *Finis.* I had that headache since I was eleven years old. How the heck did you do that?"

"Well, sir, I take no credit. Electroshock, that's the miracle worker." "No kidding. Well, I really don't remember how I got here. Will I recognize my wife and my girls? The lady fan lived next door to me?

Am I still with the Sox?"

"Look, Jim, your wife is in the waiting room. Been here every day, came from Newton, a two-hour trip back and forth. Never missed once. Quite a little lady you married. She'll be in to see you in just a few minutes." The doctor presses a buzzer, and waits for the attendant.

He turns around to face his patient. "Jim, you were ripe for a crack-up, that's all. Don't analyze this thing too much," the doctor says as the door opens up. "I'm releasing you today."

"Damn. One day I'm backing out of a limousine, crablike so that I wouldn't be recognized by anyone I stood aside, facing the big car, while the driver dug my two-suiter out of the trunk. My heart was beating a frantic tattoo on my ribs, and my head was spinning and my eyes were smarting, and the winter suit hung heavy on my saturated shoulders. My muscles ached and my mouth was dry and my throat burned and my whole body was being pulled every which way by a thousand frenetic nerve ends restlessly straining and tugging and tumbling all over each other."

"So you do remember. Oh, honey, you're getting released today!" Mary, dressed in a new red shirtwaist with red pumps and a matching bag, rushes to his bed.

"You always had a thing for men in uniform," he says, twisting, turning, then bowing in his strait jacket. "I love you in anything red."

"Jim, honey, the doctor believes you're permanently cured now of the headaches. And of course your illness."

"Hey, let a man give his wife a proper kiss today, all right?" He swoops in and gives Mary a long French kiss. After, he's aware of the taste of coins in his month, not an all-together unpleasant metallic tingle fills his empty mouth. "Look, Red, I can still do my dance." His hips sway the tiniest bit.

"You remember when I first ran out to my position; I took off my hat, waved it, and did the hula-hula in every direction? Made old Satch crazy, making monkey sounds when the great Satch was warming up on the pitcher's mound. I stole the show."

"Jim, I've kept all the clippings for you in this shoebox. Just like I know you'd want me to. Irene knows Sox fans everywhere; we collected stories around the country. Everyone worried about you, Jim. So why don't we just sit a bit and catch you up."

"Well, you got any quotes from the boss in those clips? Am I a goner or not?"

Neither is prepared for what happens next.

The news clips fly out of the box, swarm around Jim's head, settle on the floor, and stalk him. One clip stands icily apart from the others, then suspends itself and stares him down. Jimmy nods yes, yes to the clip; the first word breaks out of the gate, and with it, trailing by a hair, all the other words. One by one, they indict: Jimmy Piersall, former Birmingham Baron's outfielder, who practically tore the ballpark apart with his mad antics will never play baseball again. Now a hopeless mental patient, he will spend his life in an institution right outside Boston, the closest he'll ever get again to Fenway Park.

With a smirk, he says to his wife, "I am a goner. Gone nuts is where I've gone. Well, Mama Piersall, where to now?"

"A change of uniforms, sweetheart. Doctor says you can change as soon as you like. And then it's back home for us."

"Home. I can't remember our neighbors. Except one. That insurance salesman. Did we buy life insurance from him?"

"Joe? Irene's husband, Joe Rosenfield? I don't remember him selling insurance. It's brushes he sells. Brushes."

# 13

# Brushes with the Pa

No wonder the puppeteer has begun to back off. Who can count how many times that invisible puppeteer has had to pick up the slack on Daddy's shoulder strings. Well tough! Cut his strings. Let Daddy slump!

Daddy never sold enough insurance to put him at the Million Dollar Round Table. Go figure. The further he got from that table, the rounder he became. Now he's been asked to leave the table for good, take a hike. Good riddance to insurance; hello to helium. Up and up soars this balloon of a Daddy. He's no one's puppet now. How much further he'll go without a tether is anyone's guess. What's for sure is that he's flying solo now, not taking orders from anyone.

This is the uppest, up Daddy ever! First thing I do when I get home from Hebrew school? Search our property. I listen for his bounce or eye the sky for the great big balloon he has become. I see him occasionally. I wave. If he's waving back, I sure don't know. I search three times a week, maybe three weeks in a row.

Then, one day I wake up before dawn to the smell of paint. I go to take a pee, and find proof ... Daddy has reappeared. Fresh clues from Daddy, not Daddy himself, make their way down the bathroom door. Painted in the baby blue of our living room, with what seems to be an oversized toothbrush lying in the bathroom sink, in the lovely block print Daddy wrote in at Boys' Latin High, is a list of hard-sounding syllables. See what you make of these:

1. Neuroplectic

2. Chlorpromazine

3. Fluphenazine

4. Haloperidol

5. Loxapine

6. Molindone

7. Perphenazine

8. Thioridazine

9. Thiothixene Trifluoperazine

Wacky word endings, all zine-y and ine-y, yes, but from a list I have seen written over and over, page after page, in one of Daddy's marbled composition books from his days in Pharmacy College. I bet he made As on that test, and so he has, at last, something to show off. For whatever he has lost, he still has all ten of something—something important enough to interrupt his flight high above our home, and write them down for me. (Later, I will copy the list into my own marbled book and look them up in my *Webster's*. When I go to college, I will show my book of clues to an instructor who will send me to another. This one will say, "Ah, a simple class of medications. ("The antipsychotics.")

I forget which way to turn the knob of the bathroom door. I lock myself in twice before I open it, turn off the light, and enter the upstairs hallway, where the light is still always on to scare away the boogeyman of my little girl years.

My eyes are searchlights, moving this way and that, up and down, side to side. There, there, and there. And even there.

O God.

Four flat walls, like pages of a book, and even the back of the doors we close to save heat, all full of jaggedly printed, freshly painted words. Brushes stand dumb in a small wastebasket. On the front of my bedroom door, painted in the sunny yellow of our kitchen, only this:

"Yellow for my little Yellow Bird. XX OOO XXX," followed by a pair of lips in mid-smooch. Jesus. Daddy has given me a paint kiss, a silly, stupid paint kiss, made of poison. The wall between my parent's bedroom and mine? Another paint job; this one, "Brushes of the World":

1. Watercolor brush

2. Shaving brush

3. Chimney sweep brush

4. Easel brush

5. Niche brush - for horses only

6. Grooming brushes - people and horses!

7. Detail brushes - cars and horses!

8. Sable brush

9. Mongoose brush

10. Baby bottle brush

11. Toilet bowl brush

12. Lint brush

13. Floor brush

I don't know what to make of the Brush List. Probably part of his home-work for his new job: Fuller Brush Man. Maybe they give quizzes. Daddy had told me some pretty funny stories from his training program last month. The guys had to act out little plays—with real scripts to learn your lines—on what to say to customers who won't let you get your foot in the door.

Fuller Brush Man: Hello, Madam. I'm your friendly Fuller Brush Man, but you can call me Top Dollar Joe.

Madam: Please do come in. May I get you a glass of water?

Fuller Brush Man: Why, thank you. And for your special free gift, would you like a shoehorn or a comb?

Only Daddy raises his hand, and says, "Real people never talk like that. I am a salesman. Shall I demonstrate?"

The instructor said, "Please do, Mr. Rosenfield."

Course what he musta meant was "Please don't" and "Shut up, this is my classroom, you clown."

Too late. Daddy's up on his feet, at the head of the class. He turns to an empty chair, extends his hand, and says:

Daddy: "Hello, I'm your—"

Madam: "Look, I would buy everything in that case of yours so you can make a huge commission. Except my husband is upstairs now, and I think he's having a heart attack."

Daddy: "Oh, that so? Well, why don't I just wait here until he's had it?" (Audience laughs. Daddy bows quickly.) He performs one more skit: Daddy: "Good day, Mrs. Housewife. As you can see, I've got a suitcase full of dreck. Drain dreck to unclog your sinks and toilets, dreck shoe polish in every color with matching dreck shoe brushes. See, you'll need to shine up those lovely shoes again after you step in the dreck that overflows once the drain dreck turns to cement inside your pipes. This one's on me: an extra-large, life-sized Fuller shoehorn to pry your lazy husband's tuchus out of that ugly chair." (Woman gasps. Daddy takes his seat.)

Teacher says, "Now that you've had your fun, sir, can you kindly keep your comments to yourself?"

Not my Daddy. Never could. Which is why the small wall between my bedroom and the bathroom terrifies me. It smells like fresh Fuller shoe polish, and reads: *Yosef ben Avraham*, Joseph born of Abraham. Only three Hebrew words but giant sized. If you know Hebrew, you know this: the big-footed letters, like claws; the heavy strokes, hieroglyphics for animal names, roaring and raw; the vowels above and below—Eee! Eh! Oh!, Aye! Ah —All tiny baby cries.

These words do not belong on this surface, in this home. No, you hear the three words at shul or see them on headstones. It is how we will know our men through eternity: by their fathers. (Girls, by their mother). But I don't deserve to know my Daddy here between the brushstrokes. I hate this clue. I will not have a dead Daddy in this house. I will not.

And when I ask Daddy to please, clean up, I will say, "Start here. Here with those murderous words." Since I have seen the worst of it, I now want to see the rest, and so I head downstairs.

What's painted on the alcove on my way downstairs?

- Make it work

- Make it last

- Guarantee it, no matter what

Not bad. Fuller Brush's lifetime guarantee: "Always close with the promise." I wonder if Daddy had thought out his own final promise, but I scare myself too badly with my "wonders." Joe DiMaggio was a Fuller Brush man before he made it big. But not Joe Rosenfield. On the inside of our front door is one more message, and next to it, Daddy's sample case. Opened wide and not a product sample in sight (those me and Mom would find across the strip of land between our house and the Piersalls').

But back to the door where Daddy has traced his hands. Painted in black with a Fuller Baby Bottle Brush (stuck to yesterday's *Boston Globe* on the hallway table) the tracings zig in and zag out, covering up his failure to make the ends meet. Inside the ragged tracings, each knuckle has its letter, except, of course, for the no-account pinkies. Drawn with Mom's Poodle Pink lipstick, the block letters same as Daddy's tattooed ones. From left to right:

G-O-O-D L-U-CK

As in goodbye? As in a wish? As in a rage, as in an inside joke that cuts your own bare knuckles? I fix on my own knuckles; fill in imaginary blood-pooled letters. If I used my pinkies, a tattoo, say, "Take it back," might make for a fairer fight. Daddy hits, Daddy misses, Daddy runs, Daddy falls. Etcetera... Etcetera... Etcetera.

Damn it all. There I go crying like a little girl. Swiping at my snotty nose, I settle on the fist, the fingers, and presto! I'm back on the tattoo thing. How I'll word it in the end. How I'll have a contest for the strongest Letters in the Land, that's what I'll call it. Only I can't imagine living my whole life with the cocky, little winners: the letters that make it to the finish line—especially when two of the would-be Words of the World—"take" and "back" contain such cheap repeats: "a" and "k." Nope. "Take it back" is out. Entirely out.

And, also, because to take it back, to take it all back, where would poor Daddy begin?

I find Mom asleep again on the living room sofa. Only the sofa is not in the living room. That crazy night Daddy did all his painting, he also did some moving, putting the living room furniture in the dining room, and vice-verse. One. Silent. Night. Where did Daddy get the strength to paint, to schlep the furniture, and to lay out all those stupid Fuller Brush samples on the lawn? Did he tiptoe? Why did we need to sleep and not Daddy? Somehow me and Mom don't have the get up and go to even clean the lawn, which is half Piersall's. We've left the brushes just as they were two weeks ago. If Jimmy minds, he's not saying.

I count Mom's burnt butts in the Java and Jive ashtray that never leaves the kitchen table. Now sitting on the fancy mahogany table, this combo coffee and ciggie holder looks just as out of whack as everything else. I sit on the floor in front of the couch and wait for Mom to wake up. Even asleep, Mom's face falls together in the center, a well of waiting.

I love how one of her eyelashes is red; the other, brown. Ditto for her eyebrows. One side of Mom's hair is coppery red; the other, a light brown. This is why she's been dyeing her hair since she was a teenager. Even now what I love most about my mom is her looks. Not ashamed to say it out loud either. It's just another way God had for making her such an original.

"Oh, did I end up here again?" Mom sits up on the sofa and feels behind her for her cigarettes. "Honey, seen my lighter?"

I point to the lighter in her lap. "Why aren't we allowed to visit Daddy still? I don't have to close my eyes to see the whitest white coats, snatching up Daddy in—of all colors—his whitey white Fuller Brush Man uniform, and covering his shirt with the strait jacket. I'd probably never see the pretty, red embroidered letters spelling out Fuller Brush man on that shirt ever again.

"Come. Come and snuggle with your old lady. Is it my imagination or does the living room furniture look better in the dining room after all? I know the sofa does. Hell, let's leave it like this. What do you say, mommelah?" She gives a little laugh.

What she really inhales is her worst suspicions of her husband: His tortured soul would never find peace, no matter how he rearranged what was in his head. "I like it. Daddy hated the words together, 'living' and 'room.'"

I agree. "Once Daddy said, "who came up with this dizzy combination, living and room? If you're living in one room, then dammit, you're either in jail or in a nut house! Two live wires like us, yellow bird; we need to live it up in every room!'"

Mom's lungs fill with a thousand ways a parent can protect a child. "That was his sickness talking. He took his word games too far. He couldn't control any of it anymore. Wait. You'll see. He'll come back to us whole. Not in pieces. The stuff he's made of will once again be the glue. And he will find a place for himself. He is made of very different stuff, your Daddy." With her deepest exhale yet, she invents a happy ending, writes a different future.

I returned *Death of a Salesman* to the library last week. I don't need it anymore. I know most lines by heart:

"I'm looking for a little good news to tell your mother, because the woman has waited, and the woman has suffered…the gist of it is, I haven't got a story left in my head."

Why would Daddy always say, "I should write for radio, TV, heck, even Broadway; I've got a hundred scripts rattling around in my head."? Why say it if he was fresh out of stories?

Instead I ask, "They'll shock Daddy like they did Jimmy?"

"Daddy's at Westborough State, where Jimmy was, so I imagine he's getting the same treatment. And look, look. Look at Jimmy today."

"And he won't go back to Fuller Brush, right?"

"No, honey, they wouldn't have him. Hope the *facucktah* (screwed up) Fullers rot in hell.

See those samples rotting out on the lawn? I asked. Aren't they filled with dreck that's guaranteed to last a lifetime?

"Good. So shove them up your arse, sir," I said, "and give us some peace." She's lighting up her third cigarette already.

She is also, like me, crying.

"Mom what will Daddy do when he's out of the hospital? Start up another car lot? Be a pharmacist?"

She blows her nose, passes me the hanky. "A good blow, there."

"I will find myself a little job. It will be nice to get out. Bubbeh will come live with us. Zaydeh's been gone, going on what? Five years. You know how Bubbeh loves to cook for her family. It'll be good for all of us, you'll see."

There she goes again, wrapping me up in her love. If Bubbeh was leaving her home to live with us, Mom meant business. While Daddy would take Jimmy's place in the Violent Room of the state mental hospital, my Mom would fill Daddy's spot with her own mama.

Bubbeh's presence seemed to round all the harsh corners of our quiet rooms. First thing Bubbeh did was to scrub down all the walls and paint them over.

"When your *tahteh* comes home, he will feel at home," Bub says, scrubbing down the inside front door with a Fuller floor brush

"Ekh fah-r-SHTAT nit," I lie. Sure, I understood. I just like using Yiddish to show off.

I don't really understand Yiddish, of course, but I do love the sounds Bubbeh makes: sha-sha-sha, oy-oy-oy, feh-feh-feh, all simple and short, like Bubbeh herself. At fifty-eight, she isn't even as tall as me, a five-foot three, sixteenyear old, still growing! On account of her killer bunions, Bubbeh wobbles from side to side when she's scrubbing, just like Charlie Chaplin.

Mom asks me, "Please honey, get my mama away from the paint and give her a little air." So I walk with Bubbeh just to the end of our little street and back. The wind blows her impossibly fine hair out of place, so her scalp pokes through here and there, all pink and pearly. What a pretty, pretty head she has. In the daylight, with just a teeny breeze, land on her head, her fine little hairs become tiny threads of pink cotton candy, spinning and spinning from her beautiful pink, precious *keppie*.

She makes me want to fill myself up with Yiddish, what Daddy calls "the language of the dying and already dead." Feh on that! No one's more alive than my Bubbeh.

Ten years later, in my late twenties, I found myself living in my own tenement house. Mom had come to visit me for the weekend in Hartford, where I was teaching freshmen comp at three different colleges, and had found a nice apartment to rent. What I hadn't found yet were the storm windows, so I lit a fire in my first fireplace. In borrowed Tupperware, Mom had brought her sweet-and-sour stuffed cabbage rolls; simmering on the stove, the aroma brought Bubbeh's kitchen into mine.

"Let's get in our robes early, and hunker down for the night," Mom said. Cozier we couldn't get. Fire, check. Roasted brisket, check. Yarn and knitting needles? Check.

Couple of sweaters with necks that would never go over our heads… check. By seven p.m., we were knitting, tucked into our corners of my never-stain Herculon sofa, and had begun watching "The Movie Loft Movie of the Week."

There on the screen, in a whole new kind of black and white, a young ballplayer shouted back at the ump in this movie version of Jimmy Piersall's own book about himself. Mom watched the film without smoking a single cigarette. Even when I wafted the smoke of mine in her direction, she did not light one of her own.

A gnarly voiced, mean looking Karl Malden plays Jimmy's Daddy. The TV screen could barely restrain Malden's bulbous nose (now there's a wonderful adjective, for you). And I've waited all my life to use bulbous. When I first heard "bulbous" back when I was, say fifteen, I couldn't see why I should even add it to my "save up to use" list. With one purpose and only one—to sit itself in front of one puny noun, nose—bulbous couldn't hold to anything on my best adjectives page. Every word on my save-up-to-use list had to earn its keep.

It's the sound of Karl Malden's heavy shoes clop, clop, clopping on the screen that brought me back to the movie (I looked over and saw my mother's lips moving silently as she counted her stitches on her knitting needle). Until that movie, I'd never seen Jimmy Piersall as anyone's son. Hard-driving—relentless, really—Malden played an insatiable man who lived through his son, and pushed him headlong into his nervous breakdown. So consumed by my own, I never gave much thought to anyone else's impossible father. Not Jimmy's, and rarely my own Mom's.

"God, he had the father from hell, didn't he? Never knew that. Did you?"

Mom drops her head. "No, Jimmy and I stuck pretty much to baseball. When the press sat on Piersall about his nervous breakdown, Mr. Double Entendre of the Day, my Jimmy, said something like, 'My Daddy's the reason I'm here today.' Later, one reporter wrote: 'We can't be sure whether Mr. Piersall meant to credit the senior Mr. Piersall with his baseball career or his stay in the nut house.'"

I wondered if the Daddy on the TV was as evil as his real one. Nope.

Nothing is as lethal as the real Daddy.

# 14

# Ten Ants

Just our luck.

We'd be kissing the Green Monster goodbye a week before Jimmy would be pulling up his red sox again, suiting up for the 1953 season. What the Rosenfields would be pulling up is stakes. *Stakes, shmakes, Chrissakes.* Had to sell our house, yeah, them are the breaks. What I knew for sure back then was that I would never again babysit for the Piersalls, never get tipped as big as Jimmy tipped.

"Forget Fenway. Those bums are cursed since 1918, the same year your momma was born. Everyone says it's account of the trade. Ever since they lost Babe Ruth, they're losers period. Real losers," says Butchie, the kid from the moving company in Worcester. When "losers" pops out of his mouth, it's not the same "losers" as mine. His "e," heads straight into the "r," fattening it up, so you can't ignore the r-r-r-oa-ring R. That tells me he's a skanky Yankee lover.

As for mine? My "e" gobbles up the "r," making it a skinny shadow of its former self. Open wide: say "Ahhhhh. Looz-ah. I'm from Boston all right.

Butchie is looking straight at my two pimples. (Which is what my Mom calls my new boobies, so small that I won't be wearing a bra probably until the summer). He has some pimples himself: man boobies sit right on top of his Santa Claus belly; a load of real pimples, ripe for popping, fill his checks and forehead.

Pimples and all, I like looking at Butchie. With the help of a little grease, his dirty blond hair sweeps back at the sides, then comes together in a point at the back of his head. Point as in exclamation point, since the hair turns up over the tail: the ducktail. Maybe he likes me in a crush kind of way. Maybe I'll just have me a little crush myself. Who am I kidding?, me the Daughter of Irene the Red Sox Queen? Damn tootin', I am. No how, no way, I'd fall for a Yankee fan.

So bye bye, Buchie, skanky Yankee, from Worcester.

Except for this: the curse he left behind. The 1918 World Champion Boston Red Sox would sell Babe Ruth, the great bambino, to the skanky Yankees just one year later. Why? Some say the team needed the dough to produce a stupid Broadway play. 1918, same year Mom was born (she'd say she was put here to reverse the curse); what was to follow the loss of Babe Ruth would be at least sixty years of failures.

The Curse of the Bambino explained everything, which is why I liked the silly superstition in the first place. Another fanatical fan in the making, I was. Every lousy losing season since gave Boston something to suffer over: the curse. The air shifts slowly from muggy to crunchy and crisp. Come autumn, the maple trees start to show off their pretty colors. It's then that Bosox fans would gather up their gloom, and shout, "Wait 'til next year!" Still, I figured if the fans hadn't given up hope, had still believed the Sox could take the World Series, then maybe my own Daddy could turn his luck around, reverse his own curse, the curse of the two Daddies, Up Daddy and Down Daddy.

While my Mom waves off the moving van as it pulls away from the curb, I follow my Daddy up the stairs to our new second floor apartment. He stops just short of the door. He looks up, then down, giving it his "Daddy Dirty Look Special," so I think fast and offer up the patio, adjacent to the back entrance of the apartment door, instead. "Daddio, Daddio, let's go to the patio!" I say. The beatniks say Daddio, and me, I am feeling pretty beat.

"Who you callin' Daddio? Huh," he's asking in his clearest Up Daddy voice yet, and giving me an air jab. I can't believe I never noticed how his lips glue together, when he's like this. Has the Puppeteer snuck in, zipped up his smile, and put it away for the night?

I shut the living room door, pass through the dining room to the kitchen, and run back to look at Daddy, who is siddling up to the door, and tilting back his head. A tilt back, compliments of you know who. The Puppeteer must have followed us, hid in the moving van.

"Hey, Daddy. This apartment is the nuts! One straight line, from end to end."

He cups his eye with a pretend magnifier. He cocks his head a bit, peers down the hallway that is his life. I wonder how he sees himself through his convex lens. He takes the long view, my Daddy does, like one tiny fish sees the whole of Cape Cod.

In a whisper, he says, "Backwards we go. From homeowners to tenants. So, hey, why not live like 'em. Yes. We will live like ten, count 'em, one, two, three, four, five, six, seven, eight, nine and a-ten. Ten ants who tunnel our way through to the Promised Land!" And then he claps his hands.

"Goody, Goody!" he squeals. "Joe has put it all into motion already. Listen, my yellow bird, I called certain people, important people, people I can't name, I called them well ahead of our move. Town Manger McGrath, for one, is expecting a call from yours truly next Monday."

Not the calling again!

When Daddy was released from the hospital three weeks ago, my Mom told my Bubbeh she was worried. Worried he got out too soon, before everything was fixed up in him. Me, I worry that Up Daddy, tough bugger that he is, I worry that he has not been down. Up Daddy went into the nut house and Up Daddy came out.

Simple as that. Welcome to Worcester.

Only forty-five miles from our old place to this four-room second-floor flat in a triple-decker in Worcester, smack in the middle of Massachusetts. What came with us are the proceeds from the sale of our twelve-room brick colonial just thirty miles east, in Newton, the most affluent suburb outside Boston.

Daddy says, "Good riddance to Newton, crummy little Jew Town. Upper crust? Here you've got the pie filling, lumpy but still juicy, this center of Massachusetts. You've got the city under a town manager. A very decent man, that Francis McGrath, also a bit of a schmuck, but hey, Joe Rosenfield never shied away from any man."

He cracks his knuckles and starts to pace.

"I'm thinking maybe this house is haunted. You hear any voices?"

"No." Already I was afraid of hearing too much of Daddy talktalktalktalktalk. "What Daddy?" I already know he's shut up tight.

He gives me a long slice of silence. Had I known yet that silence was deadlier than noise? I think now that I had come to fear silence, just as surely as I had feared noise.

He's got his ear to the closed doorway of his and Mom's new bedroom. He shakes his head, goes toward the kitchen. "Honey, take a deep breath. Nah, don't. Ever ask your old lady about her beloved hometown? About how her holy slugger, Ted Williams, hit his first New England home run in Worcester. There's vision here. Wise souls are communicating all the time, maybe even right here, right now in this hallowed, haunted hall. Do you know that Worcester was once known as the shredded wheat capital of the world? Henry Perky invented shredded wheat in 1890 right here!"

Perk, shmerk, shoulda stayed a soda jerk. Like the guy who first made barbed wire in his Worcester warehouse.

This Joseph hates his new manger, that's for sure. From broadloom to linoleum. From parlor to pantry. Worse still, from huge bedrooms on their own floor to this lousy little walk-up apartment, two floors above from someone else's walk-in.

"They want perky here, I'll give 'em perky. I am a happy guy when I make up my mind to be one. And if I'm not happy here, well, hell, Worcester State Hospital is just down the street."

He speeds down the hallway, right through the kitchen, the pantry, and to the end: the back door. He leans into it and then presses his ear against it.

"I could swear I heard a high-pitched voice. Who knows? A ghost or two could liven up this party," he says, does an about-face, and picks up his pace again. "One day they will say, 'Joe Rosenfield has wheels.' I'll be running circles around those bums on the field." He picks up his pace. When he paces, Daddy's shoulders round, his head bobs down, and, right on top of his spine, a little bobbin of a knob lifts its head. (Thank you, Mr. Puppeteer. Glad you made it to Worcester in one piece). My Daddy threads his hands behind his back. That makes his dingy ribbed sleeveless undershirt pull across his chest, and pleat like a bra with nothing inside it. He's got on his white boxers with the blue diamonds and gray centers.

Backwards, of course. On his feet are black socks, and terry white slippers that belong to Mom.

"Yeah, this is capital of Nuts, too. Back in 1833—You didn't know your Daddy knew his history, huh"? He points right at me. "That's the year the first quote insane asylum unquote opened, right here, Woos-tah," making fun of the people already.

Who could miss the sound of da city? Consonants float in the clouds here. Lake Avenue is Lay Kave. The second-person pronoun? Yow-ah. Daddy already sounds like a Woostah native, clipped and fast, his speech threatens to go on and on.

"Freud himself paid a little visit during his first trip, I might add, only trip to these United States!"

"That would be where, Daddy? At Cla'k University, off Pa-kav?"

Heading down the hall, and tapping on the white stuccoed ceiling as he moves, Daddy turns to me, "You want more history?"

The thing is, I didn't.

"The first bible in the You Ess of A was printed here. Maybe the first dictionary, why don't I remember that? Uh-uh. I can't be losing dates. Not now, not ever. Never good at dating, and well, Irene." He looks up at the ceiling, cocks his head, and with his gluey tongue clucking, turns and heads toward the faucet, slurps from the spout. As he heads back toward me, he starts to sing.

"Irene, Irene, I'll see you in my dream. No, it's Goodnight Irene, Irene, goodnight. Is it, or is it the other way around? More firsts, more firsts," Daddy yells, while banging his head with his knuckles so hard and so quick, over and over, that I expect the answer to rise right through the top of his head.

It doesn't.

He commands the Daddy inside him who can still get things right. "C'mon, dummy!" More fist, more firsts. Daddy calls it with, "First ballpoint pen. First typewriter. Both invented in Worcester. Oh yeah, and you will love this one, honey, you with your great big mushy heart, you will like that the first commercial valentine was mass produced can you guess where?"

I don't like that last fact one bit. I hate fake hearts. I see Worcester like I saw Butchie. I see this city as a duck-tailed defiant who blows smoke rings just like a punk. One hand sifts an ashy mix from the south end's Wyman-Gordon, the city's steel plant, while the other hand clenches its fist around a souvenir tire from the small rubber plant on the north side. Depending on which way the wind blows, you might smell burning rubber or burning sulfur.

Worcester, Worcester, poor little sister. We lost our house, and moved here, because we had to get away, had to take Daddy away, had to bring mom back to her family here. Me, I wish I could disappear down one of this city's stupid smokestacks. I wasn't the one who lost our stupid house; I knew perfectly well where to find it.

"Do you think the fireplace works?" I ask. Perhaps I could dash up the chimney and hitch a ride back to Boston with Mr. Butchie. All of a sudden, I'm starting to miss Jimmy Piersall, and wonder if they're booing him or cheering him on his comeback. I'll know soon enough. Right now, I've got to take care of Daddy, so I take in a big gulp of air, force a great pretender's smile on my face, swipe the spit just beneath Daddy's bottom lip, and spy a fresh droplet on his nostril.

He pulls his handkerchief from his pocket, wipes his nose, pulls back his head, stares at the handkerchief, asks, "What the fuck is this thing?" and shakes his head twice.

"It's just your hanky, Daddy. Don't be scared. C'mon, blow. Good.

Again?"

"Looked like Casper the Friendly ghost there for a minute." Twice he blows, and then stuffs it back into his pocket. He tunnels toward the kitchen, the only room that can give him what he wants: a glass for his whiskey. Eyeing the boxes, he fixes on Mom's neatly printed letters: "Glassware. Fragile."

He goes for the box cutter on top of the stove. "Hey, yellow bird," he coos, "how 'bout you and me get these here boxes put away for Momma? Wouldn't that bring a smile to her face when she gets home from the store?" He's pried a juice glass from the box merely by pulling it apart and digging in.

The store he means is a dry cleaner, called White's, just three blocks from our crummy apartment, where mom is in training. She will start working there next week. Whites! It's just got be awful with a no-account color for a name, instead of family word. Even worse: she's picking up her

U-N-I-F-O-R-M today. We all know how I feel about uniforms.

Anyway, my Uncle Mucko got her the White's job. Turns out, even though she never had a job, job, my mom doesn't need to know much to work the w-h-i-t-e Formica counter, just has to promise to wear a free white smock, buy herself white nylon stockings and some pearly white nurse's shoes on account on her being all day on her feet.

But she won't complain about standing on her feet. She likes gabbing with people, trading tidbits of Sox trivia. Showing off. There's no one she can't stump, no one who knows the stats like her. I try to imagine her at the white counter. "Light blue seersucker suit, green stripped trousers, and six white collared shirts," she's say. "Starch on the collars?" she'd ask, and the customer would nod his head up and down. She may as well sing, "Whistle while you work, Adlai Stevenson's a jerk," it being a song that goes with "whyyyyyyyytes."

"Say, Mr. Dumpty, did you catch the game last night. My daughter could pitch better than that Moose." Or: "Wowzer, Mr. Dumpty. Such a handsome suit. You don't buy off the rack now, do you?" Even: "Mr. Dumpty, might you know where this stain came from?" The Mr. H. Dumpty in my mind might nod from side to side, put his head down like a little boy ashamed of a certain sort of stain, or too embarrassed to fess up. No problem for Irene the Red Sox Queen. After making her short stringy smile, she'd say, "Oh, I'll just circle this, and the cleaning crew will take it from there." Circle it, she will, with you guessed it, w-h-i-t-e chalk.

My mom, a great conversationalist, well, talking to people is what she does best. "This nodding stuff will have to go," she has said to me more than once. "Feh! Who needs another strong silent type in this world, huh? Silence? I got it in spades."

We both know she meant the silence of her own papa and my Down Daddy and his old down days. "So, Mrs. Mommy," I will ask. "What'll it be for Mr. Flubber Dubber today? Didn't I just see him head out of White Cleaners? Must've dropped something off at your white counter, yes?"

"Daddy, you want to put away the glasses first," I ask, eyeing the empty glass in his hand. Instead, he walks over the wall between the kitchen and the living room, and puts his glass to use as a listening device.

"My baby girl, my Malutch-ka-la" he says, closing in on me, hooking his empty hand around me. Right hand, his G-O-O-D, tattooed hand. "I've got to lie down on the sofa awhile. A move can kill a man."

Does he mean the move or something far worse than just coming to Worcester?

I hear the Drop Daddy Flop and see him already curled on the sofa, turning himself around, his face turned inward. One day, I will remember Daddy's face, before he turned it away from me; the face of a friendly ghost, but still and all a ghost.

Haunted he was.

Haunted by the stuff he was made of. Haunted by the bile that will rise up and burn through his esophagus. Haunted by the home he was forced to leave behind him, the failures that lie ahead of him. Haunted by what's inside his head, not sure which battery he's running on, the positive or the negative, and scared shitless he cannot control the juice. Haunted, too, by all the good luck gone bad. Haunted by the Irene of his dreams who will soon stand behind a dry cleaner's counter for a buck seventy five an hour, whose losses keep piling up, right along with his own, and haunted by me, a daughter, that won't leave him be.

Haunted, most of all, by the curse that won't reverse.

# 15

# Backwards He Ran

I was nearly twenty-five years old, for crying out loud, and I wasn't about to be cheated out of any more time. When my supervisor at the insurance company got tired enough of my fishing for corporate slogans, such as "Our goal is mediocrity seldom obtained," he conceded I might benefit from additional training at company headquarters in Chicago.

Between trips to the art institute and poetry readings, I was one busy shirker. Make that oxymoronic. I caught on quick: no training was so good that not going to it was even better. The evening's quest for the perfect mascara at Neiman Marcus paid off all right but wore me out. So while shaving my legs in an over-sized tub in my single room at the Ramada Inn, I had nearly dozed off. Not ready to give and go to bed, I eased myself out, wiped my right arm dry so as not to get electrocuted, and made a bee line for the bed.

I turned on the radio on my nightstand full blast and hop scotched back to the tub. Hoo-ha! Right leg, I said aloud, come to Mama. Your turn. As if you could find that perfect angle you had on your leg. As if that weren't annoying enough, I had this: the hippa-up-pa-pa yippa-swoosh-wush sounds from the radio. No mistaking the crazy sound of fanatics, a sound that drove Daddy out of Fenway for good. He'd said he'd heard enough from Jimmy, and besides, my Daddy claimed he could no longer abide the sound of words. Claimed, also, that he was very sensitive to noise. Get this, he said. I couldn't play the phonograph loud enough.

No matter what, tonight I was stuck with sound, just like Daddy. Shit, I thought. Not the whitey white White Sox. Not baseball, not now. But I wasn't about to run back again.

Boom. Bang. Bing.

I recognized him! It had been years since I heard his voice, but heard it I did. A roar all of its own. His voice, unmistakably his, with words made whole despite the static.

First this: "WMAQ radio. We're live at Comiskey Park where the White Sox will be taking on the Boston Red Sox. Joining me in calling the action is former star centerfielder of the Bosox himself, veteran Jim Piersall."

Then, then this, from Jimmy himself: "Well, they say if you just keep swinging, something will happen!"

But if you had just kept swinging back in the 1950s, what happened would have nothing to do with baseball, nothing at all. Whether your moods swung or hung still, whether you'd been crazy in public once too often or been crazy in private far too long, whether you lived alone in your mind or other tenants lived there with you, chances are you'd had electroshock. Who knew back then from lithium, from bipolar, bishmolar? You were mental, nuts, looney-tuned meshugenah, and that was that.

I don't know why it took me so long to ask about the perfect cure.

But it did.

"Electric shot, ma? That's what finally cured Piersall?" I had asked. As if he had had a screw loose, and somehow, it was jolted back into place.

Same place Daddy had been. Three times. "Did they hook him up to cables to, I don't know, restart his normalcy?" Thre. That was a fine college word: normalcy. Like most college words, normalcy didn't fit anything you already learned from everyday living. Restart, restart. Of course: Engine was the word I needed, as in "Restart your engines." Engine was the word a car dealer's daughter knew long before she knew who her father was, and who he was not. "Engines, Ma. I meant to say engines."

I had made her laugh. "Restart? Oh, sweetie, you'd need one hell of a jolt. Pretty horrible what they do. Put shock waves into your brain; who knows how. Some of these poor bastards have an actual fit, you know, as in epileptic fit."

"Ichkk. Sounds deadly!"

"Electroshock was a quote serendipitous unquote discovery. By some Italian psychiatrist, Guido whoever, a *meshugenah* himself, no doubt. He'd had the good fortune of watching slaughterhouse pigs get electrocuted. Not to death, but knocked out, unconscious."

I quipped, "Shit, I'm glad Jews don't eat pork. Especially now, now that I know what they do to those poor pigs."

"Exactly. They knocked the poor pigs out so it'd be easier to slit their throats. No resistance. I guess the good doctor Guido figured; why not apply the same principle to unruly human minds? It was a last resort, electroshock. If drugs didn't do any good, that's what you got. Hell, back then they claimed shock even cured psoriasis."

"And they said he was finished as a ball player!" "Feh!"

Mom's feh, a short, dense ball of a word, drove her disdain far from her lungs; the distaste bounces off the back wall of her front teeth, and over her lower lips, where she runs it down. Triumphantly, she bares her teeth, and wrinkles her nose. Caught in three letters, feh: a clipped curse on every one of Jimmy's disloyal fans, a juicy jibe at the media.

"Double feh! What did they know, huh, Ma? Huh? They didn't know our Jimmy, and they certainly never knew his Irene, the Red Sox Queen." I still used

Jimmy's nickname for her, and he still saw to it that she remained a season ticket holder. Away Jimmy, traded away more than once, mailed her six box seats for every home game at Fenway. Did it for, I don't know, like ten years.

And then it had to be me who grabbed the last bit of conversation on that phone call, and gave Mom her victory. "Ma! I know exactly what you said back then. You said, 'I hope to hell Jimmy still remembers his way back to Fenway.'"

Remember he did. Pearsall emerged from his black Caddie in the spring of '53, frisky and foul-mouthed, boasting, "I'm crazy and I've got the papers to prove it!" He didn't stay still for long and, before we knew it, he was back at work, shouting insults and fiballs for the Bosox.

While the Fenway faithful whooped and welcomed back their hero, Channel 7 followed Piersall's return with a locker room report, capturing Piersall on tape as he scooped up both his girls, Deenie and Eenie, in one arm and laughed at reporters when they asked how it felt to be back. "Ain't it obvious how I feel?" He kissed his girls over and over and over.

For months after his big comeback in the spring of 1952, and months before my Daddy's next hospitalization, I drove myself crazy trying to figure out how Piersall, who bellowed his way around the bases, suddenly shut up, went to the looney bin, and came back as good as new. Unlike Daddy, Jim found his voice again. It did not seem fair.

Unless, of course, you come to realize that maybe, just maybe, craziness wasn't about the sounds it makes but its silences. Sometimes, craziness was about silence and noise tailing each other. Trying to intimidate each other. Other times, crazy was all about an unwritten code of behavior even crazy had to honor. Like taking turns, silent mishegas stepped aside politely so noisy could have its say.

It was then, in the spring of my fourteenth year, that I forced myself into believing that Piersall may have also brought bad luck. Couldn't Piersall's craziness have crept across our lawn? Whatever had made this wild Red Sox crazy rubbed off on his next-door neighbor. And that the true curse of the Bambino was not about Babe Ruth but about Piersall. Only when the curse was lifted, and the Red Sox could take the World Series, only then would the curse be lifted and end my own Daddy's run of bad luck.

To cram for a civics test, I had shut my bedroom door early. A minute later, Daddy's knocking. "Hey, sweetheart. I don't want for you to worry." He sits down on my twin bed, and next thing I know, he is clutching my favorite stuffed animal, Geronimo Giraffe.

"I always worry about grades. Always worry." I turn back to my textbook, hoping Daddy will turn away, too.

"I guess I'll let you study then. I was worried you were worried about me. Well, don't is all I wanted to tell you. Joe is back all right. And this time, I'm connected. Well connected." Th after his final hospitalization. I lied. "That's good news, Daddy, very good news." How had I become someone I'd looked down on: a "very" person. "Very" people haven't got enough meat in their sentences, so they sandwich a "very" in, overcompensation. What? Should I remind Daddy instead of what had happened not two days before? Worcester's Town Manager, a Jewish guy to boot, had filed harassment charges against him, and threatened a restraining order. Mom stopped driving the forty miles to games, even stopped buying the Boston Glob and reading the box scores.

Daddy had made his own comeback, all right.

But it was Down Daddy who come back from Westborough State, and Up Daddy who would make him a prisoner in his own house, making sure he'd never leave home again.

Like the grimy, slimy engines I remembered seeing at Top Dollar Joe's car lot, silence would stick to Down Daddy.

Sludge, sludge would not budge. No one could get the sticky, sooty, stubborn silence off of him, out of him. Silence, *shmilence*, unholy alliance. So silence was the stuff Daddy was made of? Funny, for awhile I thought he'd been made out of booze.

Booze, I said aloud, drawing out the double O's. Boooooze. Like a spider, the word "booze" hung completely still right in front of my face. It swayed back and forth, back and forth, taunting, a Jimmy Piersall to a Yogi Berra. Jabbing, I tried to swipe it away, again and again. But I could not get the word to budge. I sidestepped that nasty spider word, and then swatted it from behind. Success!

Booze stopped dangling, stopped revolving, too, and stilled itself on top of my head. I had been afraid to inch back.

Now I had no choice but to admit I'd been wrong about craziness. The worst kind of crazy didn't make a sound. It was silence that brought Down Daddy down, down, down. Drowned Down Daddy, drowned. Down Daddy, Down Daddy, couldn't-turn-round-Daddy.

The first hospitalization: six months fewer than Jimmy's. A day after Daddy was taken out of the house by the men from the hospital, all I could think about was our lousy front lawn. How ugly the weeds were, how yellow the grass had gotten.

"Tough luck, kid, about your old man," shouts Piersall from his limo.

I pulled my first weed off the lawn. "Oh, he'll be fine. It's angina. Nothing serious."

He trots over to my front yard, stops at first, then pulls me into a bear hug. "You'll be fine, girl. And so will your old man. Look at me for Chrissakes. Going nuts was the best thing that ever happened to me! No one will forget me now, Missy Marlene. *Do you hear me?* I'm a Hall of Famer, easy."

"Hey, you, don't cry. They were real good to me in that hospital, honey. You can take my word for it your old man will be back running the bases in no time."

He ran back all right.

It was Down Daddy who went to Westborough State three more times, and a downer Daddy who came back each time. Even Mom couldn't get him to stop crying at night, when she would find him curled up in a ball on the ratty old Queen Anne's chair.

After Daddy's final, month-long hospitalization, he spoke fewer and fewer words until, one Saturday, I decided to tally up again: four words in twelve hours; one word every three hours. Amazing to me still. How I had to break him into pieces, into Up Daddy, Down Daddy, amazing. To keep my own self, that little girl in these pages, to keep her, well, sane. To make it to thirty then maybe marriage, definitely children.

All that electroshock had done such strange things. He forgot my mother's maiden name, how to cut a bagel, how to fill his Paper Mate.

And he forgot essentials, too.

Like that we had our Queenie, our ten year-old family dog. Like who was Little Yellow Bird, and who was Top Dollar Joe.

He jumped every time the phone rang. I don't know what scared him more: that someone might be calling for him, or that nobody would be asking for him.

I was living in New Haven, finishing up grad school, when my mother called me to gloat. "Jimmy Piersall went out in a blaze of glory, mommelah. That loveable crazy bastard ended up with career marks of .272 and 104 homers. Did I tell you how he celebrated his 100th homer?"

"You didn't, no." Craning my head back, I had stretched out the phone cord as far as it would go; I felt behind me for the Marlboro pack on my table, just a hair out of range. "Ma. Can you hold a sec? I gotta find my lighter."

"He ran around the bases backwards. Backwards, can you believe?

And was his manager ever pissed!"

"I can imagine. Wow." She saw through the patronizing, of course, but was too classy a lady to say so. Instead, she made up an excuse to get off the phone, apologized for having to get off so suddenly (she forgot a mah-jong date). Me, I felt like crying after we hung up. Instead, I slept in my beat-up old Red Sox sweatshirt and had a bad dream about Babe Ruth.

Piersall ran backwards.

Backwards, the very same direction my Daddy decided to travel in 1963.

Backwards he ran from third to second, taking himself all the way back to his days as Top Dollar Joe, and reselling in the rain (for cars looked so much better wet) one Peppermint Green and one Harvest Gold Chevrolet.

Backwards he ran from second to first, seating himself inside a classroom at the Massachusetts College of Pharmacy and relearning the tables of toxic compounds.

Backwards he ran to buy something at the garden supply store. Backwards he ran from first to home. Within the privacy of his home, he guzzled the better half of a gallon of Scott's Weed Killer.

Of all toxic substances, the stuff he was made of dissolved the quickest.

# EPILOGUE

If you're a Red Sox fan today, you have to figure the best players might come and go like Boston's mayflies.

But Piersall was no passing fancy. Not only did he stick with the Sox, but he stuck around so long that he became a permanent fixture in Fenway's outfield. After that, Jimmy zigzagged. But leave it to Jimmy to tally up a seventeen-year big-league career. Seventeen years, well, that's plenty of time to matter.

What also matters is how Jimmy wore his craziness proudly on his sleeve. Just like he predicted on my lawn that day, the last time I'd ever see him: players, managers, and fans alike will remember Piersall most for going nuts. No matter, that one day Casey Stengel would laud him as a better defensive outfielder than DiMaggio.

But I had Jimmy in my life longer than baseball did. And yes, he'd be a permanent fixture in my heart, since I would remember Jimmy Piersall as the Daddy who caught whatever was thrown his way, and gave his daughters one whole Daddy. Not two separate Daddies, not two characters, not two clowns called Up Daddy and Down Daddy, the men I choose to make sense of a father who made no sense.

That I had also been given the real deal for a mom may have been my ticket, after all. I figure that's why no one says, "You have only one father." What they say is, "You have only one mother."

Not two weeks after my Daddy's suicide, my mom led the charge. "Well, Marlene-zee, it's time for me to get off my tuchus, wipe off the *schmutz* from handling the dirty clothes for White Cleaners, and get myself a job. I'd shovel shit against a tide for you, I would. To get you to college."

What she did, when City Manager McGrath called with his condolences, saying Daddy was a good man but a tortured soul who could now find his peace, what she did was ask him if the City of Worcester had a place for her. It did. A free program for widows to be secretaries and get an allowance for raising the kids. Me.

She worked almost twenty-five years for the city, and then retired only to host a part-time, radio talk show on baseball. Her handle? Irene the Red Sox Queen, of course. And me, the daughter of a queen! Daddy's ability to look over a huge lot and pick out a winner had been at play no doubt when he picked my Mom on Old Orchard Beach. So there was a power hitter inside Daddy, too, for he hit one out of the park that day.

Mom often quipped, "Goddamn them Red Sox. They last won a world series the year I was born. What? Do I have to die before they win another?" No, she did not live long enough to see her boys take the 2004 World Series, but of this much I am glad: her headstone (in a conservative Jewish cemetery) is every bit as idiosyncratic: *1918-1990*

*Irene*

*The Red Sox Queen*

*Rosenfield*

Still, as I run my own bases backwards, I hear the sound of Jimmy Piersall. Sound that travels across twenty years of my life, from old Jimmy, my next door neighbor to new Jimmy, a faraway broadcaster. A voice, not unlike my own Daddy's, brings me home, and makes me a girl again.

I write because it is the only way I know to keep a voice alive.

# ACKNOWLEDGEMENTS

I am so very grateful to my many friends and family for encouraging me to press on. I'd especially like to acknowledge the never-ending love and faith of my aunt, Goody "The Great Melhado," for whom the name Goody (may she rest in peace) never seemed grand enough. Hence, I bestow the greatness.

For deft insights, advice, and peerless design, a special shout out to Lauri Baram. Also to friends Susan Costello, Susan Kosack, Chris Rogers, Kay Sherwin ... all cheerleaders extraordinaire.

And I give thanks to Rabbis Hershel Fogelman, Scott Shpeen, Nachman Simon and to Cantor Glenn Groper. No one jump starts my passion for Jewish literature quite like Rabbi Scott Shpeen of Congregation Beth Emeth in Albany, New York.

I am lucky enough to know writers to whom I am indebted. So permit me to name drop: the late, great Bernard Malamud whose critiques made me want to be so much better than I am.

To Jay McInerney, mentor and mensch, who advised me to turn the 11-page story, "Running the Bases Backwards," into this novel. "You're a long distance runner," Jay said, "not a sprinter." To Richard Ford for pushing me to "kill all the adjectives"; to Nicholas Delbanco and Hilma Wolitzer of the Bennington

Writing Workshops; to Lydia Davis, Douglas Glover, and William Kennedy of the Writers Institute at the State University of Albany for their constant support.

Finally, to my mother, Irene Rosenfield, and my maternal grandmother, my Bubbeh Bessie Goldstein, for coming before me